NIGHTINGALE

The story since 1840

NIGHTINGALE

The story since 1840

Marcus Roberts

TYMSDER PUBLISHING

First published in Great Britain in 2001 by Tymsder Publishing
P.O. Box 16039
London NW3 6WL
e-mail tymsder@aol.com
fax: 020 7372 9015

British Library Cataloguing in Publication Data
A catalogue record for this book is available from the British library

ISBN 0-9531104-5-1

Design, typesetting and production by The Studio Publishing Services Ltd,
Exeter, EX4 8JN

*This book is dedicated to Joseph N. Cohen,
Mary Nathan and David Stern in recognition of their
outstanding work on behalf of Nightingale over many
years. Gerald Lipton MBE also remembers with gratitude
the support and encouragement they have given to him as
Chairman, and, to show his appreciation has generously
sponsored the cost of publication.*

Now when you consider that all for whom we are here assembled, have reached that age which ... as our sages describe it, the hills become mountains, the neighbour's house a great distance, and we seek things we have not lost ... when you consider all this you will appreciate the great boon which our charity renders to these aged men, who, free from distracting cares find shelter, food, and raiment in an abode of calmness and retreat; who find a willing and gentle hand to diminish their natural frailties, and sympathetic hearts to revive their spirits, to brighten the evening of their life, and to enable them to attend to their religious duties – their eternal interest ...

Chief Rabbi, Nathan Marcus Adler. 1855

CONTENTS

office of the
CHIEF RABBI

Nightingale House is one of the truly great institutions of British Jewry, and we should be proud of it. Whenever I have visited I have been moved by the sheer quality and professionalism of the care it offers, and you can see the result on the faces of those who are there.

Few things are more central to Jewish values than the care of the elderly. 'Stand in the presence of age,' says the Torah, 'and honour the face of the old.' One of the most moving lines in our prayer book, taken from the book of Psalms, reads: 'Cast us not away when we grow old. As our strength fails, do not forsake us.' Societies are judged by how they treat their most valuable members: the very young and the very old. By those standards, our community is exceptional, and Nightingale House is a shining example. And what a difference it makes to its residents! It may or may not add years to their lives, but one thing is certain: it adds life to their years.

May you have continued success in all you do. May God bless you for bringing blessing to so many lives.

Jonathan Sacks

Chief Rabbi Professor Jonathan Sacks
Erev Rosh Hashana 5762

ACKNOWLEDGEMENTS

I owe a personal debt to Anne Clarke of the Jewish Resource Centre at the Roehampton Institute of Education. She put my name forward as the possible author of the book. Anne and her husband have been most helpful and supportive of my work in the past, and Anne provides an indispensable Jewish facility for South London, for Jews and non-Jews alike.

I am indebted to Daryl Green at Nightingale, who has been my main liaison with the Home. He has taken great interest in the book and has been very helpful in a myriad of ways.

Leon Smith, Nightingale's Executive Director, has been the main instigator of the project, and has made every facility available to me in my research. Leon has a deep knowledge and involvement with the Home and has helped me attain a clear understanding of what makes Nightingale a very special place and deserving of a careful history.

Many of the office staff have gone the extra mile to help smooth the path in the initial research. Photocopying a century of annual reports definitely deserves a service medal.

In the latter stages of writing the final copy, I was immeasurably helped by my friends Sue and David Wavel who selflessly provided me with quiet office space in their home to enable me to write without distraction.

I am also grateful to a number of people who have given me their time to tell me about their personal experiences of the Home, or that of their parents or relatives of yesteryear. These include David Stern who now has one of the longest associations with Nightingale of anyone living; Asher Corren, whose insights and memories as former Executive Director of the Home were essential to the last four decades covered in the book; Judith Kelly who gave me every help in researching her mother's time at the Home as Secretary. Harry Harris also gave me fascinating personal recollections of the

Home in the 1920s – he met a matron of the Home who had worked there in the 1880s – as well as information about his relative, Katie van Molen (née Harris).

Special thanks are due to Dr. Gerry Black for his assistance.

There are many others, and I thank all those not specifically mentioned whose help was equally appreciated.

Last, but absolutely not least, I would like to thank my wife, Maxine and daughter, Imogen, for putting up with the upheaval caused by such a major project – it was not easy, and writers are disagreeable company for much of the time. My daughter at nineteen months came to accept her Daddy's absence and learnt to wave me on my way with the new phrase, 'Daddy – Work'.

LIST OF ILLUSTRATIONS

Between pages 80 and 81

FOREWORD
by Leon Smith, Executive Director

Nightingale is special for a number of reasons. Born out of a charitable and humane response to the excesses of the Poor Law, it has one of the longest histories of continuous care for older people.

On the physical level it is the largest home of its type in this country and Europe. The Home has always insisted that its size is vital to enable it to offer the facilities that it has, and the quality of Jewish life it has attained. This philosophy has at times been against mainstream contemporary thinking, but has proven to be the correct course for Nightingale.

Nightingale is not a profit-making operation. It views itself strictly as a caring entity, and this has helped ensure an excellent ethos and superior facilities. The quality of life experienced by its residents, and the love shown by the staff, explain why the Home is regarded by many as probably the best in Europe; perhaps even in the world.

The Home has gained a reputation for speedily adopting innovative concepts in the care of older people, many of which were cutting edge ideas from Scandinavia. It was one of the first to introduce Occupational Therapy, and today has one of the finest arts and crafts centres of its kind.

Socially, the Home has been much loved in Anglo-Jewish Society. Many are those who have had links with the Home established through the happy stay of their own parents or relatives at Nightingale.

Though Nightingale has always been run on orthodox lines, it has been actively supported by all sections of the community. From the earliest days the charity has been backed by the Sephardi and Ashkenazi communities, and by every strata of religious observance within the community.

We now have three hundred residents. The Home is bright and vibrant, where lives are led to the full, and visitors remark on the happiness and contentment they see about them. We try to offer exactly the sort of home older people are looking for: privacy when it is needed, an abundance of leisure activities whenever they wish to be involved, and every opportunity for making real friends.

Whatever their physical state of health, we look after those in need with the most devoted and comprehensive nursing, and have special facilities for those with Alzheimer's and other forms of dementia. A panel of doctors holds regular clinics each week in our medical suite. We have our own pharmacy and dental surgery, physiotherapy and occupational therapy departments, and a large dedicated medical staff.

Helping everyone to enjoy life, countless volunteers come in every day to provide companionship and practical help. A full-time leisure activities staff organise an incredible programme of outings, musical performances, and speakers, many of them famous, on a wide range of topics. There are educational talks, religious instruction, language classes, and discussion groups. Bridge clubs, chess and other board games are encouraged. The David Clore Art & Craft Centre provides residents with the opportunity to indulge in almost any art form that interests them: pottery, painting, tapestry-work, carpet-making, knitting, sewing and much else. This huge studio can accommodate up to one hundred people at a time. For those who are less able there is an extensive programme of activities in every area of the Home. No one is left out.

We have now completed the most ambitious development programme in our history, with superb single-room accommodation and some double rooms. In Rayne House, a separate building nearby, there are twenty-four self-contained flats for those able to lead a more independent life.

The main central building is the hub around which everything revolves. It contains a modern reception foyer with the medical suite, a hairdressing salon, a large shop, and the Garden Café, a favourite meeting place throughout the year, where visitors join residents and residents relax with their friends. We have a concert hall and a beautiful synagogue.

xiv

Our size allows us to offer a much wider range of facilities than is possible in a smaller home, but we keep everything on a human scale. For example, dining rooms are small – there are twelve of them to allow for more intimate gatherings. The kitchens are fully kosher and provide a wide range of excellent food.

In addition to our residents, we also welcome others who come here each day for care and comfort, and a further group that we look after for a limited period of respite or short-term care so that their regular carers can have a break and perhaps take a holiday.

We are proud of our past, and look forward optimistically to our future.

I

INTRODUCTION

This is the first published history of Nightingale, an important and much loved charity. It is hoped that it will be of interest to the historian and the general reader; that those who have been associated with the Home will discover many new aspects about an old friend; and that this account will help to fill a gap in our understanding of an important aspect of Jewish charitable endeavour.

Nightingale had its origins in three separate charities, the Hand In Hand (founded in 1840), the Widows' Home (founded in 1843), and the Jewish Workhouse, later called the Home for Aged Jews (founded in 1871). They amalgamated in 1894, and in 1907 moved to the present site in Nightingale Lane, Wandsworth. It is now widely known as Nightingale.

All three charities started in the old Jewish quarter in the East End of London, and all were founded by successful working class men and women whose dedication and determination to alleviate the suffering of the aged Jewish poor was inspirational.

They were driven to found the charities partly as a response to the Poor Laws, which imposed draconian conditions for the distribution of poor relief, and partly in response to the conditions in the workhouses in which families were separated, sexes segregated, freedom restricted, the regime harsh and arbitrary, the diet kept at subsistence level, and the surroundings gloomy. Little or no regard was paid to the special needs of Jewish inmates whose misery was compounded by the absence of kosher food and a lack of the facilities that would enable them to perform their religious duties. Uppermost in many Jewish minds was the fear that they would die in alien surroundings. Conditions in the workhouse were an affront to Jewish values that could not be ignored, and a principal aim of all three charities was to take aged destitute Jews off the street or out of the workhouse and to place them in congenial surroundings in which their special needs were considered and catered for.

The Jewish attitude to charity differed greatly from that adopted by those responsible for enforcing Poor Law relief, and the general principle of caring for one's own was generally affirmed within the Anglo-Jewish community.

Judaism teaches that the care of the elderly is an unmistakable priority; from the principle of respect for the wisdom and experience of one's elders in general (Ethics of the Fathers), to care and respect of one's parents in particular, especially in their old age. When the Rev Dr Hermann Adler addressed the Hand in Hand in 1874 he said, "At a time when nations were sunken in barbarism, it was directed to the Jew: 'thou shalt rise up before the hoary head and respect the countenance of the aged'."

The Torah and Talmud emphasise that Charity (*Tzedakah*) and Benevolence, *gemilut hasadim*, (literally meaning 'bestowing loving kindness') are essential attributes of a Jewish life. The Talmud also teaches that the poor should be given 'sufficient for their needs', and makes clear that 'sufficient' does not equate with 'minimum'.

Unlike some other sections of the general community, the trustees of the Hand in Hand and of the Widows' Home did not blame the respectable poor for their own state. Instead they believed that the destitute aged were subject to a 'visitation of Providence' and that this was in itself deserving of compassion. The Widows' Home appeal in 1850 declared:

> It is one of the decrees of Providence that the poor shall never cease from out of the land; and it is imposed on us as a strict religious duty that we should alleviate the sorrows and afflictions to which the poor are heirs ... The law commands us to support the feeble and to protect the widow and the orphan; for if man is created in the image of God, it is that he should imitate the goodness of the Divine Creator. God is benevolent, let us be benevolent.

The charities also understood that the giving of charity in response to the visitation of Providence was an opportunity for uniting all sections of the Jewish community, spiritually and socially. One early comment on this topic, in 1845, was from the

Rev. A Levy who said, 'good can only be effected, while we remain an *am echad* (a united people); when the rich feel for the poor, the needy respect the wealthy, and each class in its proper sphere becomes a prop and support to each other'.

However the efforts of the founders of the three charities brought them into conflict with the middle class and the wealthy in the community who initially offered either adamant resistance or studied indifference. It took some time before they accepted the necessity for their existence, supported them financially, and in course of time took over their management. Their initial opposition was due to a mixture of prejudice and genuinely differing views as to how charity should be distributed and to whom. There was also to some extent a fear that such institutions, if too comfortable, might attract an influx of what they considered the wrong type of Jewish immigrant – the minority whose main aim was to come to England in order to live off the generosity of the native Jewish community.

The history of Nightingale illustrates the changing patterns of care for the elderly. In the early days, before the era of the welfare state and the introduction of old age pensions, many residents arrived at the Homes in great distress and aged by poverty and by the extremely hard lives they had endured. They would frequently spend only two or three years at the Home before their demise. The Home then saw its role as providing respite from life in the harsh outside world and smoothing the path to the next.

The move to Wandsworth coincided with innovations in the maintenance and care of the elderly. The effects of the Poor Law began to wane, and pensions were introduced. The number of the worst cases gradually declined, and the emphasis at Nightingale was placed less on direct rescue and alleviating poverty and more on improving the quality of life for residents.

The residents of today arrive not due to poverty, but in order to receive a very high quality of care they might not obtain elsewhere, and to enjoy what is by any standard a wonderful quality of life. They arrive at Nightingale at an advanced age, but still spend a considerable number of years in the Home. For many it is true to say that their years in the Home are the best of their life and, where health permits, they find a new lease of life and a whole host of new activities, hobbies and friends.

Throughout the second half of the twentieth century the Home adopted the latest innovations in old age care and today is a model of the best practice. The essential Jewish values that have been described still help define the character of the organisation, and is one reason why the Home is qualitatively different to even the best of the 'for profit' homes or state-run facilities.

II

POOR LAW REFORM AND
THE ELDERLY

There had been a general, if inadequate, system of support for the poor and elderly in England since Tudor times. The principle of 'out-relief' was established whereby a parish would make payments of money to the poor and needy living within that parish. Those who could benefit were not only the old and the sick who could not work, but also the able-bodied unemployed. Apprenticeships were found for children whose parents could not maintain them. Though inadequate to meet the needs, there was at least a rudimentary machinery in place.

Parishes became reluctant to fund other parishes' paupers, and by the 1662 Law of Settlement relief was given only in a poor person's parish of origin, unless his own parish agreed to meet the bill for maintenance wherever the parishioner was living. This made it difficult for itinerant Jews such as pedlars, and led to many anomalies.

The exact position of parish boundaries gained an exaggerated significance, especially when a pauper or his family lived on the cusp of one parish with another. In one case an unholy row broke out between two parishes because a pauper's house lay exactly on a parish boundary and they could not decide who should pay. It was adjudicated that it was the parish in which he slept that should pay, but it was discovered that his bed was also exactly on the parish boundary. It was finally settled when it was ruled that the parish where his head lay at night was to be the paying parish.

A high point of local provision was the almshouse. Some villages and a good number of towns had almshouses provided and endowed by a local benefactor for the benefit of the local poor. In addition to accommodation, clothing and a small pension were sometimes provided. The more sophisticated, such as the Whitgift Almshouses in Croydon, operated in a collegiate style with a chapel for corporate worship, and some, like the Whitgift, remain in operation today.

Though this rudimentary system of poor relief existed, it was assumed that the elderly would be cared for informally. A large family was generally the soundest form of insurance for old age. In theory, one could find the resources within one's close family for maintenance and practical care. Other than this, one might be able to call on other relatives or friends, but this was a less certain proposition.

It was generally expected that people would make proper provision for their old age. To be old, poor and suffer from infirmity or senility was among the worst of all possible states.

The system of care of the Jewish elderly largely followed the pattern of the general population, but in a Jewish context. Jews in England, as indeed in many other parts of the world, looked after their own and generally did not make a call on any other provision, even if it was available. A parliamentary ruling of 1772 established that Jews were entitled to Parish relief, but comparatively few called for it, or needed to do so.

Elderly Jews were mostly cared for by their family or friends. Where further help was needed, it was provided out of synagogue funds directed by the Beadle. In London, the different classes lived close to each other in and around the City area and worshipped together in the same synagogues. This had the advantage that the rich had a personal knowledge of the needs of the poor among them. Early in the nineteenth century, when the wealthier class started to move to the western part of London and worshipped at more distant synagogues, the classes began to lose touch with each other. When Jewish emancipation was won this also loosened the social cement that had previously bound Jews close together. Jews of every description became integrated into the English class system and adopted essentially English class distinctions. Further, the Jewish Board of Guardians, founded in 1859, and other Jewish charities, centralised the giving of charity as much as possible. They dispensed it on scientific principles, and the personal element waned.

6

The only formal institutions that existed for aged Jews before 1840 were in London, and they had wider aims than just the care of the elderly. They included *Beth Holim* (founded in 1747) a Sephardi hospital that provided for the sick poor and for lying-in women, and was also an asylum for the aged. The buildings, which still survive at Mile End, directly adjoined the Spanish and Portuguese cemetery. Eventually the Home came to concentrate purely on the elderly. It has continued until the present, but moved away from the East End in more recent times and is currently at Wembley Park.

There is some evidence of early Jewish almshouses provided by Sephardim. The tombstone of Dr. Emanuel Pacifico, who died in 1851, records that he devoted part of his property to building almshouses.

There was also the Jews' Hospital, *Neve Zedik*, (the '*Abode of Righteousness*'), founded in Mile End in 1807 'for the relief of imbecile aged and the educating to useful industry of the Jewish Poor'. The hospital was established with assets of £30,000 stock yielding £900 income a year, from a fund originally collected by Abraham Goldsmid. Asher Goldsmid, also of banking fame, was Chairman. The Jews' Hospital was intended for the reception of five aged men, five women, and ten boys and eight girls. Over time, it concentrated on children to the exclusion of the old, and amalgamated with the Jews' Orphan Asylum. The old were eventually boarded out and given financial support when the Asylum moved to Norwood in 1866, as the old people found that the new home was too far out from town.

There was one early, if short lived, charity that provided pensions for widows. The 'Holy Society for the Adequate Maintenance for Widows and Orphans' was founded in 1788. Beneficiaries had to be genuinely needful, of good character, and not play cards. The society was founded by ordinary lay people as a self-help society and was funded by small subscriptions. Those who were already members or related to members had first call on the benefits of the society.

It should be emphasised that these organisations provided for small numbers only. Furthermore, the Jews' Hospital did not cater for Jews from the lowest strata of the Jewish poor – their candidates had usually fallen on hard times having previously enjoyed a more happy estate, rather than having been in that condition all of their working lives. It was not a self-help society, and was administered by members of the Jewish establishment.

From 1795, an increasingly large Jewish under-class existed in London, mainly the result of the immigration of poor Askenazim from Western Europe. Unemployment and under-employment were endemic among them – for reasons of religious scruple, prejudice against Jews, lack of trade skills, and continuing immigration. Eventually a huge tranche of London's Ashkenazi Jews fell dependent on Jewish charity to make ends meet, but it took time for charitable efforts to catch up with the needs of a large pauper population.

Changes to the Poor Law in 1834 created a crisis in care for the elderly, Jews and non-Jews alike. The new principles that were adopted were designed to ensure that only the truly desperate would apply for poor relief and even then, perhaps, might think twice about it. It was argued that indiscriminate relief demoralised the beneficiaries. Inmates of the workhouses were maintained at a level below that of the lowest paid workers, the so-called principle of 'less eligibility'.

Charles Dickens portrayed the despair of the workhouse in vivid and ironic terms. He averred that the members of the Boards of Guardians convinced themselves that the poor really liked the conditions:

> So they established the rule that all the poor people should have the alternative ... of being starved by a gradual process in the house, or by a quick one out of it. With this view they contracted out with the water-works to lay on unlimited supplies of water; and with a corn-factor to supply periodically small quantities of oat-meal; and issued three meals of this gruel a day, with an onion twice a week, and half a roll on Sundays.

The horrors of the workhouses remained etched into folk memory even until comparatively recent times. As a young boy I was often told how the local elderly people still shuddered at the very mention of the workhouse.

While the prospect of having to enter the workhouse would strike fear into prospective Christian inmates, it would have created terror among Jews who found themselves in that position. Jews faced serious additional problems within the workhouse ethos, and felt alienated. The nineteenth century workhouse made it almost impossible for a Jew to carry on a full Jewish religious life. Only non-kosher food was provided, and there were no facilities to celebrate the Sabbath and the Festivals.

Those who attempted to carry out their religious practices experienced active hostility and derision from other inmates and from the workhouse authorities. Pesach was a particularly difficult time. Some Jewish inmates took their chances and went outside the workhouse for the duration of the festival until poverty forced them back in again at its end. With the best of intentions, the Jewish authorities followed this practice of withdrawing inmates and putting them into temporary accommodation during Pesach. To the modern eye this was psychologically cruel and unjust. While contemporary reports made no comment on the justice of the strategy, they made no recommendation for it either. Some of the most pious elderly refused to compromise their religious practice and ate only bread and drank only water; starvation was nearly inevitable.

The worst prospect for Jews residing in the workhouse was the end of it. Many aged poor died there after only a short stay. For too many years the Jewish community countenanced the deaths of fellow Jews alone among unsympathetic strangers, without the comforts of Jewish faith, and with the sure knowledge that the final insult would be burial in an unmarked Christian pauper's grave.

The situation was made worse because many of the Jewish middle and upper classes seemed genuinely or wantonly ignorant of this shortfall in charity. Looking back at this period, in 1876, the *Jewish Chronicle* editorialised:

> It was the general opinion among the Jews until within the last few years, that their needy co-religionists were helped, supported and placed beyond absolute want, from the time when they issued from the cradle to that when they entered into the grave. The discovery, real or supposed, announced by members of the humbler classes of a hiatus in the chain of Jewish charity, was therefore regarded with doubt and at first received with little favour by those accustomed to support Jewish institutions.

The Jewish establishment made attempts to formulate an

effective, corporate, Jewish response to the problems caused by the massively expanding Jewish underclass and the new harsh law that consigned increasing numbers of Jews to the untender mercies of the workhouse, but found it very difficult in practice to help Jewish inmates by negotiating an amelioration of their conditions. There seemed to be a general communal reluctance to deal with the most destitute Jews, and this applied even to children, as the Jews' Hospital refused to take them from the workhouse until pressurised to do so by the Jewish Board of Guardians, in 1868.

The Jewish population of London increased fourfold during the first half of the nineteenth century. Given that the Jews' Hospital was for long the only old peoples' home and had not increased its intake, there was clearly a pressing need for additional provision to be made.

Tired of waiting, working class Jews decided to help themselves, and found their own alternatives to the workhouse.

III

CREATION OF THE HAND IN HAND ASYLUM AND THE WIDOWS' HOME

The Hand in Hand and the Widows' Home were grass roots charities formed by working class men and women for the relief of distress among their own class. They felt that as the Jews' Hospital did not cater for the emerging class of impoverished and aged Jews at the lowest end of the scale, there was a need for a new general institution to house them.

The 'Hand in Hand Asylum for Decayed Tradesmen' was founded in 1840, close to Dukes Place, and accepted 'the aged, the infirm, and reduced Jewish tradesmen'. As far as can be established from varying reports in the *Jewish Chronicle*, it started when the founders rescued a destitute, shivering and starving ninety-year old man from a door-step, a gentleman known for his highly respectable character whose religious principles would not condescend to let him beg, steal, or go to the workhouse. The founders informally collected a penny subscription for him, and later provided a room. He was soon joined by a second pensioner, and then followed by others from the workhouse and the street. The original lodging became the nucleus of the Asylum.

Details of the early days of the Hand in Hand rest on oral history. If the charity had been founded after the deliberations of a committee the facts might have been recorded in writing at the time, but they were not. Reliance has to be placed on anecdotal reports in the *Jewish Chronicle*. This makes it difficult to distinguish who did (or did not do) what, as there are confusions caused by inaccuracy of recall. Also the epithet 'founder' in the *Jewish Chronicle* is sometimes used loosely, even inaccurately.

In September, 1845, when the Chief Rabbi, Dr Nathan Marcus Adler, visited the Hand in Hand to accept the offer of becoming the official patron of the Society, Joseph Pyke gave him the following account of the foundation:

> This institution owes its origins to the energies of the humble class of our brethren, who, when the toils of the day were over, met, as was their custom, to spend a few hours in a neighbouring house. A very poor man bereft of relatives, and of the means of providing himself with the common necessities of life, introduced himself to their notice, confiding to them the secret that so long he had worn in his breast; touched with pity at the sad tale he told, they relieved him, and endeavoured from week to week to allow their friend a weekly sum, and immediately commenced a subscription to carry their object into effect, which with the blessing of Divine Providence and the assistance they received, enabled them to place another object of pity on their little fund. Time rolled on, and their success progressively increased, so that they were able to take the lower part of the house adjoining this present asylum, [in St James' Place off Duke's Place] and place there their charge, for such it was, bestowed on them by our All Powerful Creator. From year to year, they were enabled to add another and another individual to receive the benefit of this society. The Committee ascertained that one of our brethren had (by reversal of fortune) been compelled to seek shelter in a 'Union Workhouse,' which was derogatory to our holy religion. Through the assistance of some valuable friends (many of whom are present), he was placed in a position to take him thence, and placed in a path whereby he was enabled to return to his creed and to his God. The individual alluded to is still an inmate; we have at the present time six male pensioners.

Mr. Israel Isaacs of Swan Street, one of the Committee, also offered the following insights into the conditions of the men they relieved. He said that the Society afforded the old men, 'a home and a shelter. They were wandering about houseless, and without food or clothing sufficient to protect their aged limbs against the inclemency of the winter's blast; or, as has often been the case, been compelled to seek refuge in the Union Workhouse, and forced to eat forbidden meats, etc, and could only offer up their daily prayers to Heaven, amidst the scoffers of religion'.

The rate books show that in 1843 the Home was at No. 5 Duke's Place, a house in which a box maker carried on his business in the basement. At some point after 1843, and certainly by 1845, it moved to the house next door. It then moved to 22 Jewry Street in

1850, to Wellclose Square in 1854, and finally to Well Street, Hackney in 1878.

Accommodation in the Home was simple, quite spartan, and somewhat cramped, and located in insalubrious surroundings. The Wellclose Square home was larger and much better appointed than its predecessors, and included a small synagogue. In the 1850s that area had declined, but still enjoyed a gentility retained from the time the rich and titled inhabited its spacious environs. The *Jewish Chronicle* of 6 February 1868 described the Home in the following terms:

> He (Mr. Montefiore) visited the institution the other day in company with its honorary officers, and he could not refrain from expressing the admiration which he felt, at the order and regularity which seemed to pervade every part of the establishment. Although there was an entire absence of luxury, yet an air of comfort and cleanliness surrounded the building, which appeared to be peculiarly fitting to its inmates. In one of the rooms he saw some fifteen or sixteen men, the youngest being about sixty-three and oldest ninety-four. They appeared happy and contented, and were loud in their exclamations of gratitude to those gentlemen who had so unceasingly laboured for their support and well being.

The key founding members were a Sephardi, a Mr. M. Mendoza, and an Ashkenazi, a Mr M. Lazarus, a notable cooperation for the time. This theme of Sephardi and Askenazi cooperation in the Society continued, and for many years there were leading Sephardic officials in the society. Mr. Salomon Pool, a long-standing treasurer, was of Dutch origin and a *parnassim* (welfare official) of the Sephardi Synagogue. His brother, Marcus, was a Warden of the Ashkenazi Great Synagogue.

At the 1859 Annual Dinner, Louis Nathan pinpointed the essential difference between the Hand in Hand and the Jews' Hospital. He observed that, 'there was a peculiar feature in the Asylum which distinguished it from the Jews' Hospital':

> The latter, as known, is a refuge for those who have once seen better days. In fact, this was one of the primary objects for which it was established. The Hand in Hand Asylum, on the other hand is intended for those who have never seen better days – in fact, whose best days are those spent in the institution. It is for the toil-worn mechanic, the old clothesman, and all those persons who honestly yet in poverty struggle through life, and whose whole life is a protracted starvation. It is right

that the broken-down tradesman should in his old age be provided for, such is the mission of the Jews' Hospital, but it is equally desirable that those who have never broken down, because they had never risen in life, should be cared for; such is the object of the Hand in Hand Asylum.

The earliest known document relating to the charity, a property tax document of 1843, names a Mendoza as the Trustee. M. Lazarus was the first treasurer.

An important founder member was Israel Isaacs, a butcher of 34 Dukes Street, who was President in 1843. Isaacs was an elderly man himself, a fact often alluded to in reports of the time. It seems that due to the pressures of making a living, he was able to turn his greatest efforts to charitable matters only later in life. One of the long-term supporters and patrons of the charity was the well-known Rev. A. L. Green (1821–83). Born of humble parents in Middlesex Street, he became noted for raising the status of Jewish clergymen and as a major force in Jewish charitable provision and its reform. Green said that Isaacs was one of his patrons in early life and that he owed his position in life to him. A similar honour, as a founder, goes to Jonas Jacobs.

The story of the Widows' Home followed a similar pattern. It was founded in 1843 at the instigation of the Chief Rabbi, Dr Nathan Marcus Adler. The aim of the charity, as later described in the *Jewish Chronicle* by Mr I. L. Meirs, was 'the withdrawal from Christian Workhouses of such of our helpless sisters in faith, who had, by dint of poverty, been compelled to seek such shelter', and indeed the founders' first act was to rescue widows from the workhouse:

> A few humane persons at once snatched these wretched creatures from the workhouse, and by great earnestness of purpose, established an asylum for them, where they pass the remainder of their days as cheerfully and happily as their forlorn condition will admit of.

Another motive for the formation of the charity was to prevent Jewish widows from dying out of contact with members of their own faith, 'for there was little consolation to be found on the death-bed of the sincere Jewess, resigning her spirit amidst those who had no sympathy in her anxiety of having those of her creed around her'.

Premises were acquired at 22 Mitre Street, close by Bevis Marks

14

and the Great Synagogue. The first collection in support of the institution totalled a mere two shillings!

By December 1844, the Society had rescued and offered shelter to six women, 'of whom four had been extracted from Christian workhouses, and two had been elected inmates by the votes of the subscribers'. Three had died, and three were still resident at the Home. By 1851, fourteen widows had become inmates, of whom eight came from the workhouse and the rest admitted from 'extreme distress'. Most of the widows had had protracted periods wandering the streets before they sought the last resort of the workhouse.

The founders were Abraham Green, who was elected as the first President of the charity, and a Mr. Woolf. Green was a significant charitable activist within the community. Of Dutch origins, he lived in Middlesex Street (Petticoat Lane) in Aldgate, and was well-known as a street vendor of cucumbers and olives. During the cholera epidemic of 1830 he helped found the Jews' Orphan Asylum, now part of Norwood Ravenswood. It is related that during the terrible epidemic he found three young orphan children on the street. Seeing their predicament, he took up two of the children in his arms, led a third by the hand, and went about the Jewish quarter with his cucumber bowl until he had collected a small maintenance fund for them. Green was one of the most active members of a fourteen-strong local committee set up to deal with the problem. The Orphan Asylum was officially founded in Leman Street in 1831. In course of time Green became President of the Widows' Home, the Hand in Hand, the Lying-in Charity, and the Widows' Pension Fund. As will be related later, his son, S. A. Green was also to play a vital historical role as the founder, in 1871, of the Jewish Workhouse, the forerunner of Nightingale.

Mr. Solomon Abrahams was another key figure. He intervened at an early crisis in the Society's fortunes 'when the question arose as to whether (from want of funds) their project should be abandoned. At that juncture he, Mr. A. had voluntarily dubbed himself President, had taken it upon himself to organise a committee, and, aided by a loan of £50 from the Treasurer [Mr. E. Jacobs], had brought the institution to a successful pass'.

The founders were substantially helped and encouraged by a Mr.

S. Dias, presumably another Sephardi. The first Secretary was Joseph Mitchell who became the proprietor of the *Jewish Chronicle* in 1844.

Considerable endurance and persistence had been required to establish the Society. Mr. Abrahams modestly claimed that, 'All he could take credit for was tenacity; for amidst all the difficulties of the charity he yet clung to it as a drowning man to a plank'. Mr. Woolf added that, ' . . . the difficulties the founders had to contend with could hardly be conceived'.

Some of the widows were rescued in the most pathetic circumstances. In 1850, a Mrs. Cohen:

> An aged and imbecile widow was found late at night in the street and carried by the policeman on duty before the magistrate of Worship Street Police Court on Wednesday last. The few pounds found on her person the result of a legacy (and not of begging, as erroneously stated by the public journals) have been handed over to the Asylum, on condition of sheltering and protecting her during the remainder of her life.

The Asylum made an appeal for funds using Mrs. Cohen's example and added that, 'numbers of aged widows are prowling about our streets eking out a miserable existence by casual charity'.

Another case, in 1858, was that of 'Bluma Joseph, a destitute widow, without friends or relatives in a position to assist her, who was obliged to have recourse to Whitechapel workhouse, where she lived for several months:

> As Passover approached, her religious feeling would not allow her to transgress the important precepts connected with Israel's great festival. She left the workhouse, but immediately after, destitution compelled her to return, when luckily for her, she was discovered by a member of the committee, through whose interposition she will now be enabled to end her days in comfort, with her conscience made easy, and her religion in peace with her God.

The Widows' Home virtually shadowed the Hand in Hand in its series of moves. From 22 Mitre Street it moved to 19 Duke Street in 1850, and then to 67 Great Prescott Street, Goodmans Fields, in 1857. Finally, in 1880, it moved to Hackney, immediately next door to the Hand in Hand.

Both charities (and indeed a number of others like them) were

(II) *A parrot was introduced in the men's sitting room in the 1920s.*

(I) *34–37 Stepney Green. The home of the Jewish Workhouse 1876–1907.*

Ferndale. *View across the gardens in 1907.*

(III)

(IV)   *'Ninety-seven, bless her'.*   (V)   *'Quite well, thank you'.*

(VI)   *'A thousand years between us'.*   (VII)   *'Sammy'.*

(VIII)   *Enjoying the fresh air of Wandsworth.*

(IX)   *Men and women had separate sitting rooms.*

A CHORUS OF PRAISE.

The Chief Rabbi.

Very delighted with this beautiful and comfortable Home.

Mrs. Adler.

This Home is certainly a perfect institution. The comfort of the inmates has evidently been the one thought for all connected with this palatial building,

The Right Hon. Herbert Samuel, M.P.

Much impressed.

The "Jewish Chronicle."

Are the inmates happy? You have only to look at them to be convinced that they are as cheerful a set of old people as you will meet in any institution.

The "Wandsworth Borough News."

A perfect haven.

Mrs. A. Sebag-Montefiore.

Perfect.

Mr. F. Haden Ferguson.

After what I have seen here my only regret is that I am not a Jew, so that in my old age I might hope to end my days here.

Mr. Stuart M. Samuel, M P.

A true haven.

The Rev. G. J Emanuel (Birmingham).

Delighted with all I have seen.

Mr. S G. Asher.

A model Home, beautifully kept.

Mr. J. R. Cattle, J.P.

An example to all other communities. The management reflects the greatest credit upon the Master and Matrons.

Dr. J. Edwards (Jamaica).

Exceedingly pleased with my visit to this institution. Everything in perfect order. Reflects great credit on the management.

Mr. Samuel Gompers (Washington, U.S.A.)

Splendid.

Lady Spielmann.

The Home is most perfectly kept, and all look very happy in it.

Mrs. D. Lloyd-George.

Beautiful Home.

Dr. E. W. Hamilton.

Magnificent!

Mr. George Storey .

A model Home, unsurpassed for comfort and cleanliness.

Admiring comments of visitors, 1909.

(X)

(XI) *Residents assisting the staff in the kitchen.*

(XII) *State of the art when installed, the boiler was salvaged from the war damaged laundry in 1944.*

(XIII) *Mrs Helena de Niet, Matron and Mrs Rege Breuer, Lady Superintendent, in early 1930s.*

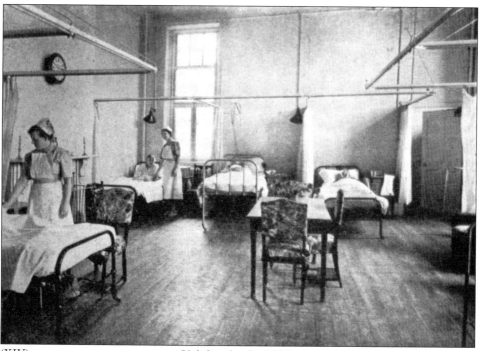

(XIV) *Sick bay in the 1930s.*

Fundraising dinner at the Savoy Hotel, 1932.

(XV)

created by small groups of working class Jews out of spontaneous acts of kindness. Initially, funds were raised informally. It was only later when the founders formalised their efforts and became official charities introducing an effective, continuing collection of funds and improved administration, that they were able to extend their good works.

The founders were for the most part successful, established, and moderately prosperous shop-keepers and tradesmen – grocers, greengrocers, clothes salesmen and butchers. They were generally neighbours who also worked close by, and set up their charities a few doors away from their homes. It would be reasonable to assume that the foundation of the charities flowed from existing friendships and their local social, economic, and religious networks.

The Homes accepted only old people judged to be of 'good character', and what the Victorian era called the 'deserving Poor'. It is unlikely that they would have countenanced accepting those who were wilfully destitute.

It seems that if there were any tests of Jewish eligibility these were applied informally. The issue of who was a Jew was easier to establish then than it is today, and the criteria were apparently far less doctrinaire. However it was clear that for both institutions an important motive of rescue was religious, to enable Jews to affirm their Jewish faith and to die in the faith.

The Homes were primarily intended for candidates without exceptional health problems or incapacity, though there are some references to the Widows' Home taking in 'deserving bed-ridden widows', and there were some infirm men in the Hand in Hand. It was expected that the elderly would breathe their last in the Homes.

IV

THE CHARACTER OF THE HOMES

The Hand in Hand and Widows' Home were essentially similar in origins, character and ultimate development. While these working class charities were formed from the most Jewish of charitable instincts, and to address a specifically Jewish predicament arising within a general problem of poverty, they were conventionally Victorian in structure.

They copied the standard 'penny society' Victorian model that would have been instantly recognised by most contemporaries. Penny societies were working class, self-help societies. They were eleemosynary in character, raising funds for their activities through subscribers giving small regular amounts, hence the 'pennies'.

It was not entirely disinterested charity, but a mixture of charity and self-insurance. Subscribers gained voting rights in return for their support and that enabled them to vote on the admission of new inmates. It gave them a lively interest in the activities of the Society, and it meant that they could promote their own preferred candidates for benefits. Further, subscribing to the society would entitle them to be considered for admission themselves.

Their main virtue was also their vice; the voting structure could be an undignified procedure, and one that did not always result in the most deserving candidates being given a place. To obtain the necessary votes, candidates had to prosecute an almost political campaign to muster the necessary support. Frequently advertisements would be placed in the papers by leading supporters of one candidate or other.

This fault of the Victorian Penny Societies was widely recognised and subject to continuing pressure for reform. The middle classes opposed them not only because of the voting system, but because the societies in some forms could be construed as encouraging the poor to gamble. For example, there were some societies whose subscribers could draw for lots entitling them to supplies of coal or other provisions if they were successful, a form of lottery. If one takes a more Marxist view, their virtue was arguably the way in which they empowered the working classes and helped engender a greater class cohesion.

In terms of administration, the Hand in Hand and Widows' Asylum were run by a small number of paid officials, and were governed by a committee that met periodically. The day-to-day organisation was directed by a House Steward or Stewards and a Matron. An early House Steward of the Hand in Hand was Lewis Isaacs, a former pupil of the Jews' Free School, who served in his post assiduously for many years, certainly from around the 1850s and into the 1870s. He was helped in the 1850s by the Matron, Mrs. Magnus, and her husband. In 1854 he was assisted by a Mr. Barnet.

While the main funding was by subscriptions, these did not cover all their financial needs. Both societies found that they needed to hold a regular Annual Festival or celebratory dinner to promote the society and raise funds. These were usually held in taverns, coffee houses, or assembly rooms. For example, the 1849 anniversary supper of the Hand in Hand was held at Howard's Coffee-House, and the 1850 Annual Festival at the White Hart Tavern, Bishopsgate. The Annual Dinner of the Widows' Home in 1851 was held at Lazarus' Assembly Rooms (a Jewish venue) in Mansell Street, Goodman's Fields.

These occasions were atmospheric, and became increasingly grand as more wealthy guests and patrons were drawn to the charities. The 1851 Widows' Home dinner is a valuable example in that the reporter on that occasion described the setting for the dinner, as well as the proceedings. 'The rooms were adorned in a pleasing and graceful style, the principal decoration being a banner placed behind the chair bearing the words, 'Success to the Widows' Home'. The supper was provided by S. M. Lazarus, and '... was of a sumptuous description, and gave the greatest of satisfaction'. There were musical entertainments, and 'the hilarity of the evening was increased by various well-executed pieces of music by Mr. Saqui on the pianoforte, and by Messrs. John Collins, sen. and jun., and Samuel Collins as vocalists...'

The main business was conducted during the meal. There was a lengthy series of toasts, with speeches largely of a patriotic nature or complimentary to the committee and major patrons. At the dinner described above, there were toasts to the Queen, Her Majesty's Consort Prince Albert, the health of the Rev. Dr. Adler, Success to the Widows' Home (the main toast), the health of the President, Mr. S. Abrahams, the Corporation of the City of London, the Vice-President Mr Silva, the Treasurer Mr E. Jacobs, the Honorary Secretary and the Committee, the Press (the *Jewish Chronicle*), Mr. Samuel Goldsmid and the Stewards (the gentlemen who had volunteered to bring in their wealthy friends to support the Society's dinner that year), the visitors, and the Sub-Committee. It is hardly a surprise to learn that the company was detained by the celebrations to 'a late hour'.

The Homes held other periodic fundraising events to make up their shortfall. The Widows' Home held one disastrous excursion to the still new wonders of Crystal Palace in 1855 that was completely rained off, and had to be repeated a week later. The use of sales and bazaars were also a regular recourse later on in the century. The Homes occasionally dabbled in theatrical speculation to raise funds.

Over time, the charities received legacies that were used to purchase stocks and annuities which provided a more stable form of income. Many of these stocks were in railway companies or foreign bonds.

It is important to emphasise that the primary function of the Homes was to be a literal refuge or asylum, to save the aged poor from starvation and exposure on the streets or the terrible conditions of the workhouses. Their secondary function was to allow the residents to practice and die in their faith. Many of the early inmates did not spend a long time in the Homes, so that the Homes had something of the character of hospices.

Nonetheless, the Homes had some residents who attained great longevity. Several centenarians are mentioned in the annals of the Homes, one of whom was 103 years of age and in command of his faculties. Though early death was a feature of nineteenth century life, my study of the cemeteries of London and Kent suggest that there was a strong phenomenon of Jewish longevity, especially in stable and established communities, with unusually large numbers surviving to reach their century.

The Homes were not planned, as they are now, with the stimulation of residents as a main objective. This was to be a much later development and concern. Old age was largely seen as decline, as an antechamber to death, and charity was effected by 'smoothing the pillow' of the dying. The Chief Rabbi, Dr Adler, during his visit to the Hand in Hand in 1855, gave an eloquent account of the problems and requirements of old age. He explained why an asylum was so valuable:

> Gentlemen we all know that old age is a season of feebleness and infirmities. Now when you consider that all for whom we are here assembled, have reached that age at which ... as our sages describe it, the hills become mountains, the neighbour's house a great distance, and we seek things we have not lost. When you consider that the load of old age becomes still heavier when want and distress are added to the burden, and care, attention, and solicitude are wanting; when you consider that the aged must feel the distress peculiar to that season the deeper when they have seen better days, and acted their part with integrity and honour; when domestic happiness does not cheer their heart; when former beams of hope to receive some return from children have disappointed them; when year after year deprives them of some friend, or steals away somewhat from their little store of comfort; when you consider all this, you will appreciate the great boon which our charity renders to these aged men, who, free from distracting cares, find shelter, food, and raiment in an abode of calmness and retreat; who find a willing and gentle hand to diminish their natural frailties, and sympathetic hearts to revive their spirits, to brighten the evening of their life, and to enable them to attend to their religious duties – their eternal interest.

The Homes were simple but clean, and the main daily activity consisted in sitting around the fire in the sitting room, punctuated by meals and religious observance. Over the decades the problem of the old people quarrelling with each other is frequently mentioned. But residents retained a degree of autonomy, at least to the extent that they organised and held their own religious services.

As time passed, activities were provided for the residents. There were periodic treats and meals on festivals or to celebrate events in the lives of the committee. One of the more distinctive customs was the Purim treat or dinner that was provided for the residents of the

Hand in Hand. This was initiated by Mr. Israel Isaacs in memory of his mother, who had always sponsored a dinner at Purim. He had continued the same custom according to her wishes, and said he hoped that after his death his children would do the same in his name. The Widows' Home also had Purim treats; in 1853 it was a substantial dinner of '...roast veal, etc., and almond pudding...', typical fare on special occasions. Later, occasional outings were introduced. While the daily routine was limited, the atmosphere in the Homes was generally described as cheerful.

The main difference between the two Homes was that the Widows' Home was less fashionable. It took a long time for it to build up anything like the patronage of the rich or to match the subscriptions of the Hand in Hand, and there was some talk of a rivalry between the two.

V

POLITICS, EMANCIPATION
AND THE HOMES

One of the more surprising aspects of the history of the Hand in Hand and The Widows' Home was the role they played in the on-going struggle and agitation for Jewish Emancipation. This was not without precedent. In the earlier part of the nineteenth century the Jews' Hospital was closely linked to the emancipation movement of its time and to key non conformist groups in the City. At least half of its membership and subscribers were members of the 'Royal House' group which consisted of political liberals, the most important merchants in the city, wealthy Nonconformists, and Quakers who were agitating for the removal of political disabilities.

During the crucial episodes in the struggle for Jewish freedoms the Hand in Hand and the Widows' Home were used as an informal political platform for reformers and their allies based in the Corporation of London. The Corporation regularly petitioned Parliament for the removal of Jewish disabilities. Two primary players, Baron Rothschild and Alderman Salomons, were patrons and supporters of the Hand in Hand Society. In the 1850s the issue of the thwarted admission of these two gentlemen to Parliament became a central issue. Rothschild was elected to Parliament as early as 1847, but like Salomons, who was elected in 1851, found that as a Jew he could not take the Parliamentary oath. The Annual dinners, attended by many prominent non-Jews, provided a forum in which pro-emancipation speeches could be made and press coverage obtained.

In June 1854, the Hand in Hand held a dinner that was notable for the impressive ranks of the rich and powerful arrayed at the tables. The chief Jewish and Christian guests were not only distinguished and of the highest rank, but were all foremost campaigners for the Jewish cause.

In the Chair was B. S. Phillips, a merchant who, in 1846, became the first Jew ever to be returned as a member of Common Council. A strong supporter of the charity, it was he who was largely responsible for attracting such prominent figures to the dinner. Present were the Lord Mayor, Alderman Sir James Duke, MP; Alderman and Sheriff, David Wire; Sir John Key, the City Chamberlain; and Sir Anthony de Rothschild. Both Baron L. de Rothschild and Salomons had consented to attend the dinner but were unavoidably absent, as was Sir Moses Montefiore.

In his speech, the Mayor said that he felt legal restrictions on Jews should be removed:

> The sooner such laws are abolished, the better for the honour of this country. The first vote I ever gave in the House of Commons was in favour of Jewish Emancipation, and I have also voted for my honourable friends, Baron Rothschild and Alderman Salomons, to take their seats to which they have been elected by the voices of their constituents (*cheers*). As a native of this country, I consider we labour under deserved reproach whilst there are laws which exclude these gentlemen from their just places.

These were stirring words of support. Sir James Duke, another powerful advocate of Jewish emancipation, described how he had presented a petition to the House for the removal of Jewish disabilities, accompanied in his efforts by the Sheriffs, Sir Moses Montefiore and Alderman Salomons. He urged the Jews to continue to press for reform and spoke of the high character of Salomons as well as all Jews in general who had served in office. He also praised the Jewish community for their respect for the laws of the land.

Sir John Key was honoured by mention of the fact that it was he, one of the longest-standing reformers of the City of London, who moved in the Court of Aldermen that Salomons should be permitted to take his seat in the next court without signing the declaration then required.

Similar speeches were made on other such occasions, and they had a cumulative effect. Emancipation for Jews was finally won in 1858, and the predecessors of Nightingale House played an important role in the most crucial political episode of modern Anglo-Jewish history.

One may only surmise how the comparatively humble founders of the Homes must have felt when their station in life suddenly shifted, as they presided at meetings attended by some of the most powerful people in the land. Sometimes the committees were forgotten in the heat of the celebration. At the Hand in Hand dinner in 1855, Jonas Jacobs had to interject a forgotten toast in honour of the founder, Israel Isaacs, to which omission the *Jewish Chronicle* added the laconic rider, '– a toast, which, no doubt had been forgotten among the number on the list.' Perhaps they were relieved when it was back to business as usual.

VI

CRISIS, RESISTANCE AND
GROWTH 1850–1870

The following decades set severe challenges to the prosperity of the two charities, and at times to their very existence. In the first seven years of its operation, the Widows' Home had a total income of £900 of which £800 came in small subscriptions of weekly pence from the 'humbler classes'. In 1852, an average year, only £62 was raised in subscriptions and a further £74 by the Annual Dinner. Annual expenditure was usually in excess of income, and both charities were hard hit by local trade recessions. The Homes initially responded by digging deeper into the personal resources of the committees, and then by recruiting middle-class charitable men on to their committees to turn things around.

In 1853, the Widow's Home held a joint fundraising event with the Laying-in Charity, as they had done in previous years. This was chaired by Nathan Defries, another middle-class philanthropist. Also at the meeting was Sampson Samuel, who greatly helped the Hand in Hand that year. Samuel was one of the first Jewish solicitors – a respectable and undoubtedly middle class profession. The event was successful, and it was noteworthy that nearly all the donations were made by members of the middle-classes. In a comparatively short period the Society had managed to widen the social basis of its support, though they had not as yet persuaded any of the very wealthy to join them. The effect of this widened support was that donations doubled compared to the previous year.

In 1854 Isaac Lyon, described as 'middle class', took over the reins of the Hand in Hand from the veteran Israel Isaacs who, it would seem, stepped aside to allow a more vigorous response to the financial crisis. That year the Society won over Jonas Jacobs, who became a Vice-President, and Sampson Samuel. Their combined efforts were vital. Sampson was described as the 'stepping-stone' who had brought the attention of the Society to the wealthy.

Benjamin Phillips persuaded Arthur Cohen, the young son of the broker Benjamin Cohen, to chair the Hand in Hand fundraising dinner of 1854. Cohen was a great success, and had evidently taken his brief seriously and investigated the facts. He made a forthright and impassioned plea for the Home, directly criticising the rich for their indifference, or even direct antipathy, to the cause, on the sole basis that the charity was too small or should be amalgamated. He pointed out that many of them happily supported the Jews' Hospital which had exactly the same scale of provision as the Hand in Hand. He also reminded them of their absolute duty to relieve suffering and not to ignore the already existing and valuable instruments of charity. He said that the Hand in Hand had no fundamental objections to a suitable amalgamation.

He also addressed the issue of class prejudice, saying that what lay behind the objections was often a sentiment, '...indicated by the popular advice – "throw not pearls unto –", well, then, unto animals I will not further define than by explaining they are neither attractive in appearance or aesthetic in deportment.' He concluded by linking the cause of emancipation and civilisation with the cause of Jewish charity.

Both Cohen and Phillips became long term friends of the Hand in Hand and promoted it for nearly two decades. They also continued to ensure the attendance of a goodly collection of the 'great and the good' at the Society dinners over the years. At the 1869 dinner, F. D. Goldsmid, H. Faudel, and significantly, Frederick Mocatta were present, as were H. L. Keeling and Saul Isaacs. Keeling was the first professing Jew ever to be elected a church warden. Isaacs was a leading figure in the patriotic volunteer movement, a colliery owner, as well as being the Member of Parliament for Nottingham. In 1870 the guest list included Henry Hart, the Mayor of Canterbury, Alderman Emanuel of Southampton, Baron de Stern, and Chief Rabbi Artom of the Sephardi community.

The advances made during the 1850s ensured the continuity of both homes. However there was an increasing divergence in the fortunes of the charities. The Widows' Home remained, comparatively speaking, a Cinderella relation. Its capital in 1876 consisted of stock to the value of £860; by this time the Hand in Hand had amassed a total of £3,620 stock. While both became more stable and prosperous, the Hand in Hand attracted a wealthier patronage and far out-paced its younger sister. At one appeal function of the Widow's Home the rueful, if not bitter, comment was made, 'Does benevolence hang back because, forsooth, no aristocratic name parades in the list of the committee? ... and yet there is the melancholy fact staring us in the face, that the Widows' Home ... is yet least supported and permitted to struggle on in the most extraordinary circumstances'.

Pressure was exerted on the Societies to amalgamate. Amalgamation of charitable efforts, following 'scientific' principles, was one of the great, irresistible, historical concepts of the era, similar to the 'free-market' in our own time. The idea was regarded as self-evidently true by its advocates, who were many. 'Amalgamation' was a shibboleth of the Jewish Establishment, and the *Jewish Chronicle* carried frequent campaigning articles supporting the principle, exhorting organisations such as the Hand in Hand, Widows' Home and Jews' Hospital to unite and avoid duplication of efforts.

It was undoubtedly true that the vastly increased demand for charitable support was a strong argument for a rational provision of help, if it was to be afforded by a community with finite means. The Jewish Board of Guardians, founded in 1859, became a major influence, and it applied consistent pressure towards amalgamation and charitable reforms. The *Jewish Chronicle* looked to the precedent of the French Jews who had centralised their charities and managed to make their resources work more effectively than the English.

However, amalgamating institutions that had only superficially similar aims was never to be a simple affair. The Widows' Home and Hand in Hand were right to claim that they were distinctive and fulfilled very specific needs. Also there could be no guarantee that the economies of scale predicted by the amalgamationists would be as striking as claimed because the two charities were being run efficiently and economically.

For a time the Jewish Board of Guardians was hostile to the Homes. It held the view that every effort had to be made to prevent immigration by those whose main aim was to live on relief. The charities, on the other hand, were concerned only to distribute help according to need. This lead to a period of conflict.

The issue of class conflict seems to have been at play, as suggested in Arthur Cohen's remarks at the dinner. There were also issues of social politics at work, as the Jewish establishment was determined to deter the feared tide of destitute immigrants coming to draw on the largesse of Anglo-Jewish charities. They were concerned about the potential cost, a prime concern for the Jewish Board of Guardians, and also by the fear that it would rock the delicate status quo built up between the Jews and the host nation over many decades. Jews had readily adopted prevailing Christian notions of the 'deserving poor' and English notions of class distinction.

There was a general pattern of interference in the work of the working class charities by the wealthy classes. All too often, charities instigated by the poor were taken over by the rich once they had become successful, despite the previous opposition to them. The later foundation of the Jews' Temporary Shelter by Simon Cohen is a classic case for comparison with the Hand in Hand, the Widows' Home, and the Jewish Workhouse. Cohen's early shelter, opened by him to provide accommodation for destitute, newly arrived immigrants, was founded in 1879 and set up in virtually identical circumstances to the old people's homes. He ran it for six years and received encouragement from the Chief Rabbi and General Booth who admired his work. His charity was not supported or recognised by the rich, though F. D. Mocatta was an exception.

Attempts were made to pressurise Cohen to close down. Eventually the sanitary inspector issued a closure notice. It reopened in 1886 in new premises, 'under new management' as it were, with funds provided by 'a few gentlemen in the West End'.

A takeover had been brutally effected, and Cohen had been ousted. Even though he was included in the general committee that was appointed, he was just one of many, and the First Report of the Home, though not doubting his good intentions, was in fact brutally disparaging of his efforts to help the foreigners:

> It will be clearly shown that the shelter [the new one] was established to supersede, and has effectually superseded, an objectionable and long-

existing refuge, and has subsequently led to the closing of private resorts that were beyond question a scandal to the community.

The clergy harboured a persistent and general suspicion as to the motives of the rich. The rabbinate valued the work carried on in Cohen's Shelter, and did not share the views of the Jewish establishment. At the later foundation of the London Jewish Hospital, in 1919, the epitome of a working class movement, the Haham, Moses Gaster, delivered a speech in which he warned the supporters of the Hospital, 'Beware the Rich!'. He told them not to be lured by large donations of the rich, as this would all too soon lead to the charity being effectively taken over. The Hospital was notable for the resistance it met from community leaders when it was proposed, and the Haham was no doubt aware that 'the cousinhood were capable of passing seamlessly from opposition to support, and of taking over the reins of control'.

Eventually the Jewish Board of Guardians came to appreciate the value of the charities, as the Homes were fulfilling objectives that would otherwise have fallen upon the Board to fund and organise. The Board, unwilling to incorporate the burden into its remit, eventually adopted a collaborative role.

As the century progressed the Jewish community experienced a radical shift in its social and demographic landscape. What had been a constant but growing stream of Jewish immigration over the century became a vast unceasing tide after 1880 that continued until World War I.

This mass of usually destitute and desperate humanity vastly increased the need for community charitable provision. The dislocation of entire communities, and not least families, brought many who had no-one or nothing to fall back on should ill-fortune strike. In a period of a few years there was to be an entirely new clientele of the aged poor for the Societies to deal with.

By 1872, the Jewish Board of Guardians had adopted the policy of discouraging the foundation of new, separate, Jewish institutions, where it was not deemed strictly necessary. This led them to oppose any idea of a separate Jewish Workhouse, even though the increase in poverty dictated it. Solomon Green was shortly to step into the arena and create a furore with his proposals for a Jewish workhouse.

VII

THE CREATION OF THE JEWISH WORKHOUSE 1871–1874

Solomon A. Green (1830–99) was the leader of the movement to create a specifically Jewish workhouse for the aged. Solomon, known as 'Sholey'. was the son of Abraham Green, who was one of the founders of the Widows' Home and a worker for the Hand in Hand, the Lying-in Charity, and the Widows' Pension Fund. Green followed his father's calling as an East End trader and emulated his father's charitable work. Of impulsive nature, he was always ready to support a needy cause.

There had been a continuing increase in Jewish destitution in general, but particularly among the elderly. Many more Jews were falling outside the charitable provisions made by the community, and they found themselves having to enter the workhouse, both in London (especially the East End) and in the provinces. This included children, adults and the elderly. At the time the community was either unaware of the scandalous situation, or ignoring it.

What made the problem more acute was that some workhouse inmates were at the very bottom of the Jewish under-class, and were generally less likely to be eligible for what help was available. It is important to remember that when the poor are mentioned in the Jewish context, that the working classes were eminently conscious of differences in status within their own class. Simon Cohen called the foreign paupers he helped 'the out-cast poor'.

A further dimension related to the origins of the poor. When Green eventually established his home most of its inmates were of Eastern European origin, whereas the Hand in Hand and the Widows' Home had a high proportion of inmates who were of Dutch or German origin, or were native born. This suggests that Green was in part addressing a problem linked to the more recent immigration of the foreign poor.

Green knew that the attempts that had been made by the Jewish establishment to moderate conditions in the workhouse had not been effective. He also accepted that he would have to overcome a general refusal within the community to admit that there was any shortfall in communal charity provision.

He began his campaign in the 1860s when he privately supported three old people taken from a workhouse. In 1864, he conceived the idea of establishing a separate Jewish workhouse. However it was not until 1870 that he was in a position formally to propose the establishment of a Home. He approached the Jewish Board of Guardians to gain their help, but they harshly refused to see him. He asked the Poor Law Commissioners for help, but no grant was forthcoming from the Parish Unions. To add to his woes, he met even more resistance from the Jewish leaders he approached.

Lesser men might have conceded defeat at this point, but not Green. Instead, he decided to start the Home on his own, recruiting help and subscriptions from those who were willing to assist, which was largely his fellow working class, men such as Julius Solomons, a cap maker resident in England from before 1868. Two public meetings were held in 1871. The first, on 19 February 1871, at Princelet Street Synagogue was poorly attended, but at least it yielded a resolution that there should be a Jewish workhouse. A further meeting was called for 10 March.

The first meeting led to a very public contest between 'Nemo', a highly regarded and supremely influential columnist and letter writer to the *Jewish Chronicle*, and Green and his supporters. 'Nemo' was the pseudonym of his cousin the Rev. A. L. Green, who in a letter to the *Jewish Chronicle* on 3 March, argued vehemently against the provision of a Jewish Workhouse and made extremely offensive comments. He branded Sholey Green and his supporters as 'ignorant' and 'irreligious'.

At the second meeting Sholey, speaking equally forthrightly, revealed the identity of 'Nemo' and made comments that according to the *Jewish Chronicle* were 'abusive' about 'Nemo'. It is difficult to ascertain exactly what was said, but it is beyond doubt that

Sholey was at least in part a victim of editorial bias by the *Jewish Chronicle.*

There is an almost schoolboy conspiratorial air about his 'alleged' uncovering of 'Nemo'. The paper wrote, 'He then requested the honorary secretary to read a letter bearing a *nom de plume* ... on the 'Workhouse Question' and he proceeded to attack the eminent writer in severe terms. He even went so far as to pretend that he knew the author, which we declare is an impossibility; and his guess is particularly amusing to those in the secret'. In fact, Sholey was right. A large part of the following report was then spent on reporting the speeches that were made by those defending 'Nemo' and little on the main business of the meeting.

Only a few years later, in 1876, the *Jewish Chronicle* admitted there had been bias in the treatment of Green. They wrote in an account of the history of the Home:

> It appears to us that a certain bitterness and personality were unnecessarily imported into the discussion, and that ungenerous remarks were passed on the promoters of the scheme by a very few writers, who perhaps only meant to display the supposed smartness and pungency of their style.

The second meeting enabled Green to proceed, but at the cost of alienating public support among the rich.

He had been adamant at the meeting that a separate Jewish workhouse was the only solution to the problem, and informed those attending that there were twenty-three elderly Jews in workhouses in need of this help.

On the basis of small subscriptions from working class supporters, and an offer of accommodation at a run-down house at 123 Wentworth Street, Green proceeded with his plan. Wentworth Street was in an unsavoury area of Spitalfields that was to be the scene of one of the notorious Ripper murders in 1881. Valiant efforts were made to make the property fit for its purpose.

Initially, fourteen inmates were admitted, in triumph, in time for Pesach 1871, a great liberation from the exile of the workhouse. What was more, within a very short time 1,900 small subscribers were enlisted. The new Jewish Workhouse attempted to get the parish unions, from which the new inmates were extracted, to pay the customary subsidy, representing the money they were bound to pay for maintaining the individual. The unions were not to be persuaded, until the Kingston-upon-Hull Union accepted the principle and made a grant. This represented an important breakthrough.

The workhouse proved a struggle to sustain. It became clear that support from the wealthy was essential for its survival. Green sought to rebuild his bridges with his potential patrons, even those who had opposed his attempts to establish the Home.

He went some way to achieving this in 1874 when he persuaded the giant of Jewish charity administration, Frederick Mocatta, to become involved. Mocatta was a banker who had retired early with a substantial fortune. This enabled him to engage in philanthropic endeavours and he became directly involved with the running of more than two hundred charities. Mocatta had the power and influence to make the charity a lasting success.

Furthermore, Green was brave enough to make relevant apologies in the press for his previously intemperate remarks. This encouraged renewed (but still limited) interest in the charity by the wealthy in the community.

Mocatta fulfilled his promise to help, when later that year he effected a reconciliation between the Home and the Jewish Board of Guardians. The organisations sent reciprocal delegates to each other's meetings to aid cooperation, an arrangement that proved very effective and benefitted both sides.

Mocatta encouraged Green to reform the constitution of the Home to allow for non-workhouse candidates to be admitted, because he felt it was unjust to insist on prior residence in a workhouse as a condition of entry. The ridiculous situation had arisen whereby needy individuals entered the workhouse for a day simply in order to qualify for entry. However, some of the most principled and deserving candidates refused to enter the work-house. This particularly applied to the very religious. The constitution was changed to cover this, and the new name, 'Jewish Home for Aged Jews' was adopted to reflect the change.

Sholey resigned in favour of Mocatta, who took up the office of President of the Home. Green became President of the House

Committee. Barrow Emanuel, Ernest Louis Franklin, (the banker) and Wolfe Isaacs were made Vice-Presidents. They were supported by a general committee, a House committee, an investigating committee, and a finance committee. Green retained an active and respected involvement in the running of the Home until he died in 1899. The change in the management of the Home proved critical for its survival and success, and achieved the best conditions for the inmates. Insofar as this was another charitable takeover by the wealthy, it was conducted on mutually agreed and equitable terms.

In 1876, the Home moved to 37–9 Stepney Green, premises provided by Mocatta. There were two very large houses made into one. Built in 1694, and the oldest building in the area, it had originally been occupied by very wealthy people. It had spacious rooms and wide stairways and corridors, as well as some surviving touches of grandeur. There was a 250 feet garden extending to the rear that was partly used as a vegetable garden to help feed the residents, a tradition that was to continue there, and subsequently at Nightingale House, until the end of the Second World War. A new wing was added to increase the capacity to a maximum of fifty residents.

The managers worked assiduously, and by the end of the 1870s had raised income to £1,400 per year, spending about £950 a year on its thirty-five residents. Their average age was seventy-four, and it cost 10s 6d per week to maintain each of them. Mocatta made a gift of the property to the Society – a vital gift that helped secure the future of the Home. It remained in Stepney Green until the move to Wandsworth in 1907.

Mocatta had made it a condition of his help that the voting laws of the charity had to be changed, to end the old voting system with all its inequalities, and to allow a committee to choose the inmates instead. This committee sent out visitors to assess applicants for the Home on a consistent set of criteria, and they reported back to the committee who then made their decisions at set times of the year as to who would be accepted for entry. This was a much fairer system. No longer was balloting a form of patronage in which knowing the rich and prominent was the only safe way to secure a place. It is still the basis of the modern system of entry to the Home. Mocatta's contribution was so important that it would be accurate to describe him as the 'second founder' of the Home. The change in voting rights carried with it a further fundamental change to the charity. It removed the direct participation of the working class subscribers in the running of the charity, and their contribution to the Home's income became proportionately less.

VIII

AMALGAMATION AND CONSOLIDATION

The committees of the Hand in Hand and the Widows' Home had long been convinced of the benefits that could be derived from a merger, but they were held back by the views of their rank and file subscribers. The committee members smoothed the path to constitutional union by arranging for the two Homes to move next door to each other in Hackney, into properties that could easily be physically linked and made into one. This was a shrewd decision. If an amalgamation was to be effected, there would be no emotional issues raised by one home having to 'surrender a property', or move wholesale to another, with a consequent loss of identity.

The Hand in Hand moved to 23 Well Street, Hackney in 1878 after its old lease fell through. The new freehold cost £865. Extensive modernisation plans to 'model' specifications were carried out under the direction of the Jewish architect, N. S. Joseph, and the facilities included a synagogue. Whilst the work was being done the residents were housed temporarily in the recently vacated former Jews' Orphan Asylum building at St Mark Street, Goodman's Fields.

The Widows' Home moved next door in 1880 after building new premises, with every modern amenity, on the site. The plot cost £5000 and the buildings £1,300. Four years later the two homes amalgamated. Moses Davis, the treasurer of the Hand in Hand, played an important part in this new departure and was responsible for the eventual merger with the Jewish Home.

Davis (b. 1849) was an interesting man. He was the grandson of Joel Hart, one of the founders of the Jews' Orphan Asylum. He had an extensive career in charitable work with a wide involvement in many other Jewish charities. He was a founder of the Jewish Home for Incurables, and assisted in the formation of the East London Tenants' Protection Committee. He was the Vice-president of the Old Ford Hebrew and Religion Classes, was on the committee of the Stepney Jewish schools, was a member of the Board of the East London Synagogue, and vice President of the Bromley and Bow Institute, and of the Bow and Bromley Conservative Association. He was also a founder and Honorary Secretary of the Notting Hill Synagogue and the Beatrice Girls' Club. He was a wonderful asset to have on your committee.

Once the Hand in Hand and the Widows' Home were one, there was a general expectation that they would unite with the Jewish Home for the Aged before too long. However, there were important divisions amongst the poorer classes. There was resistance from those who felt that respectable retired tradesmen and widows should not have to consort with paupers. But amalgamation was inevitable given the success of the Jewish Home and the economic realities that conspired against the continued survival of smaller homes. The charities, prodded by Davis, united constitutionally in 1894, and were now collectively styled as the 'Home for Aged Jews', though they remained split between the sites in Hackney and Stepney Green.

F. D. Mocatta was elected President of the merged Home. The vice-presidents were Ernest L. Franklin, Barrow Emanuel and Wolfe Isaacs. The treasurers were Henry M. Harris and Richard H. Raphael. They were supported by an executive committee, a house committee, an investigating committee and a finance committee. The stated aim was 'to provide a Home for, maintain and clothe, aged respectable and indigent persons of the Jewish Religion, who shall have attained the age of sixty years, and shall have been resident in England for at least seven years'. Interestingly, in view of the earlier discussions about the benefits of economy of scale, it was to be many years before the single unit operated more cheaply than the three individual societies.

In 1896, there were a total of 105 individuals in the combined institutions, 56 men, 33 women, and 3 married couples. There were a further 10 paying inmates, who were housed in a special wing built at Mocatta's expense at the Hackney Home. The Committee was grateful that the number of paying residents was increasing, and pointed out that no difference whatsoever was shown between the treatment of paying and non-paying residents. 'It shows a sense of independence on the part of those who do not require charity, and speaks highly for the efficient management of the Home'. The overwhelming majority of inmates were in their sixties and seventies, a few in their eighties, and two in their nineties. The average age of death was eighty.

By the end of the nineteenth century the Jewish Home and Beth Holim were no longer the only Jewish Homes. There were a number of almshouses founded by Abraham Lyon Moses, Henry Moses (1838), Joel Emanuel (1840), and also the Miriam Moses and Jacob Moses Alms Houses (1862).

The various non-residential pension societies that had existed alongside the London homes from an early date continued and expanded their work. The Aged Needy Society (founded in 1829) maintained eighty-six pensioners in 1880, paying them the respectable sum of five shillings per week. Other Societies included the Aged Destitute Society, the Helping Hand Pension Society, and the Society for Relief of Widows.

IX

THE MOVE TO WANDSWORTH

It was long mooted that the Jewish Home should move out of the East End into healthier surroundings, provided that a reasonably cheap and accessible property could be found. The existing premises were becoming increasingly unsuitable in terms of accommodation and sanitary arrangements. The Committee accordingly searched for a suitable building plot. In 1903 the Home contracted to buy a plot of land at Stamford Hill (near the Home for Incurables). A deposit of £320 was paid to the vendor, a Mr. Button. In 1904, shortly before the contract was due to be completed, there was a dramatic new development. In honour of his parents, Sydney James Stern, Lord Wandsworth, offered the Home a residence called 'Ferndale', with two and a half acres of land at Nightingale Lane, near Wandsworth Common. He had purchased it for £5,200.

Sydney James Stern (1844–1912) was an assimilated English Jew deeply integrated into the English establishment. He was an aristocrat, and had lordly estates at Hengrave Hall, near Bury St Edmund's, and at Bolney, Sussex, in addition to a town house in Mayfair. He had estates of up to 2,000 acres in extent, and owned freehold property in the county of London. He was Honorary Colonel of the 4th Volunteer Battalion of the East Surrey Regiment, and a Justice of the Peace for Surrey and London. Educated at Magdelene College, Cambridge, he was admitted to the Inner Temple in 1874. He did not practise at the Bar, but entered the family banking business. In 1891 he became the Member of Parliament for the Stowmarket Division of Suffolk, and was elevated to the Peerage in 1895 in recognition of his financial services to the Liberal party. He was remarkable for being in every respect an English gentleman of the classic hunting, shooting, and fishing persuasion. He was also a member of the Royal Yacht Squadron and of the Four in Hand Club. Though he maintained a life-long interest in Jewish affairs, his involvement with the Home appears to be one of his few, if not his only, contribution to Jewish charities.

It seems clear that Lord Wandsworth never intended to live in the house, and that he bought it for charitable purposes. His choice of the Home for Aged Jews as the beneficiary appears to have been due to the 'persistent advocacy' of Rabbi Isaac Samuel, the Honorary Secretary of the Jews' Deaf and Dumb Home which was already in Nightingale Lane and whose President was Lord Wandsworth's brother, Sir Edward Stern.

Following the gift of *Ferndale*, the Charity Commissioners blocked completion of the purchase of the property in Stamford Hill. The trustees rescinded the Stamford Hill contract and asked for its deposit back. The matter went to the High Court and the Home won resoundingly against the unfortunate Mr Button. However subsequent reports suggest that despite their judgement the Home did not recover the money.

The stage was set for a great refurbishment and redevelopment of *Ferndale*, so that at last the two sites of the Jewish Home could be united and their residents live in the most suitable environment possible. *Ferndale* was a luxurious dwelling. The first Jewish residents, fresh from the East End of London must have found the location and the surroundings strange.

Early in the nineteenth century the present day site of *Ferndale*, now Nightingale, was part of a six acre field, bordered on one side by Nightingale Lane, and on another, by a watercourse. As the century progressed the field alongside the lane was split into three and sold to a new set of landowners. The area was being developed speculatively for the wealthy, with villas in miniature landed estates in what was a healthy attractive area, close to London. By 1865 houses had been built on the site, some very substantial, with semi-circular carriage drives to the front door. There were four trees at the front of one house which were the old elm trees that for many years dominated the frontage of Nightingale House.

One of the more notable local builders and developers, George Jennings, built himself a house on a substantial scale. This new house, that he named *Ferndale*, was in an ornate Italian villa style, faced with Bath stone and terracotta dressings, and crowned with a

41

dominating campanile tower over a hundred feet high. The building was on three stories with a basement. There were nine principal bedrooms and two nurseries. On the ground floor was a morning room, library, billiard room, conservatory, drawing room, and dining room, and domestic offices including the kitchen and scullery. The basement was mainly used for storing wine, but also housed a furnace and the boiler rooms.

The gardens were extensive and would become replete with all of the features that might be found on a gentleman's estate. There was a conservatory with an artificial stream issuing out of it into the grounds, a double vinery, two ferneries, an orchid house, a peach house, a melon house, a walled kitchen garden, forcing pits (probably for forcing home-grown pineapples), a terrace, and two fishponds, one of which was substantially planted with more ferns. There was even a raised plantation of holly trees, reached by a flight of steps, which added a distinctively eighteenth century feature to the grounds.

The name *Ferndale* was almost certainly given because of the multitude of ferns cultivated at the house as well as its location in a slight declivity. The mass cultivation of ferns was a late-Victorian, horticultural passion yet to return to public favour.

The last owners of the house, before it was purchased by Lord Wandsworth, were the Cramer family who were rich merchants with connections to British Honduras. It is possible that the family were of Jewish origins, though equally they could have been of German Christian stock.

It was evident that exhaustive alterations would have to be carried out to convert the house for its new use. The Charity Commissioners procrastinated on the legal formalities. Detailed plans were eventually drawn up by the architect W. Flockart to the most modern specifications, but that scheme proved to be too expensive. It was decided that they would have to settle for the 'simplest and least expensive character of work and materials suitable to a building of its class'. The plans were modified several times to cut costs by about £10,000, and eventually Messrs Johnson & Co of Belle Vue Rd, Wandsworth were chosen to complete the works at an agreed price of £17,000.

In July 1906, Lord Wandsworth laid the foundation stone for a new wing at a ceremony, organised by Isaac Samuel, at which the Chief Rabbi was present. The Bayswater Synagogue Choir provided the music. Fifteen months later, the initial work was completed and the Home was provided with a mortuary. In October and November of 1907 the inmates were transferred to their new home in brakes – a memorable journey for the old people. There was a private consecration service a few days later.

Two additional wings with accommodation for married couples were included in the refurbishment; the Adelaide Franklin Wing funded by her children, and the Hannah Davis Wing (1909) paid for by her husband Isaac Davis, the Vice-President of the Home. Davis also endowed this wing with £5,000 of Indian Railway Stock, and made other generous donations to the general funds of the Home.

Finally, on 26 June 1910 Lord Wandsworth officially opened the completed institution. He said he was proud of the manner in which his gift had been utilised by the community, and he donated a further £1,000. He was made Honorary President of the Home in recognition of his munificence. A garden party followed the opening. A commemoration tablet made by Harris and Son of 216 Mile End Road for the sum of £9.14.0d recorded the event and is still preserved in the Home.

By 1911, Nightingale had 147 residents. Innovations included the then new-fangled electric light, an electric lift, a new infirmary for chronically infirm women, and a modern laundry. In one month in 1909 the laundry dealt with 5,516 pieces, sufficient for one change of clothing a week for each inmate. Later photographs of the laundry apparatus reveal a machine of quite lethal appearance.

Another innovation was the adoption of a new accounting method known as the 'Three Hospitals Funds'. It was used to make comparative analyses of expenditure with other similar organisations.

In 1901, the Committee took the bold decision to appoint five women to the General Committee as Lady Governors, and in 1907 a Ladies' Committee was established. Miss Sarah Magnus, of whom more will be said later, who was already a Lady Governor, served on this committee too. The belief was held that women would be better able to contribute to the supervision and running of the domestic arrangements in the Home if they also had a formal role in its administration.

The 1896 Annual Report revealed that subscriptions and donations were falling. Following the move to Wandsworth, the Home was physically severed from the East End from which the majority of new residents came. This, together with the reforms that had been introduced into the voting constitution of the Home, seem to a great extent to have been the cause of this falling away of individual subscriptions. It seems likely that the working class, the grass roots supporters, felt they no longer had a direct involvement. Subscriptions were always a comparatively minor part of the Home's total income, and before 1940 never exceeded £700 in any year.

This decline in income was more than made up by the creation of Aid Societies that were to prove essential for the future prosperity of the charity. The appropriately named Mr. Cash and Mr. Lotery were of considerable assistance in fundraising efforts, respectively as chairman of the Aid Society and organiser of fundraising entertainments.

A chapter in the history of Nightingale was symbolically closed with the passing of Lord Wandsworth in 1912. He left an estate of £1,488,610, worth about £60m. today. His parting gift to the home was a legacy of £5,000. He was buried at the Balls Pond Road cemetery of the Reform Synagogue.

Isaac Davis died in the same year. Unfortunately, he did not live to witness the unveiling ceremony of a bust of himself by Mr Alfred Drury A.R.A., privately paid for by the Committee. It has been placed in a prominent position as a memorial to him.

X

LIFE AT NIGHTINGALE 1904–1912

At the turn of the nineteenth century Nightingale had an essentially Victorian institutional ethos. The residents were called 'inmates' and were treated as the 'objects' of its charity. New admissions were expected to enter the Home with little more than the clothes that they arrived in. Contemporary photographs show residents in rooms bare of personal possessions, or at best a few scant photographs and small effects. Male inmates were required to attend synagogue and wear a kappel, (skull cap), a regulation that was maintained into the early 1960s. Most, apart from married couples, were accommodated in wards and dormitories. They were not meant to have any income, and they were not given any pocket money until 1921. Not surprisingly, apathy was a problem as well as quarrelling among inmates.

Inmates' movements were restricted, and the fitter among them were expected to engage in unpaid daily chores to help clean and maintain the Home. Some sixty residents were engaged in this work in 1910, and others were also deployed in a workroom in the Home, probably engaging in activities that could be described as occupational therapy before its time, though not then regarded as such. One spirited lady, a certain Mrs. A. Rosenthal, did not let age dull her spirit and she insisted that she should be paid for any work that she did for the Home. This *chutzpahdick* and revolutionary suggestion seems to have shocked the Committee, but it was not until 1922 that the Home conceded the point and granted small allowances. Similar allowances were made to residents who were utterly destitute. Mrs Rosenthal eventually left the Home of her own accord saying that she could work.

Activities were still largely restricted to the segregated men's and ladies' sitting-rooms, where secular and religious reading material and the usual parlour games were provided. The women engaged in knitting, sewing and crocheting to keep themselves busy. The men's sitting room had a parrot in a large cage which was much appreciated. Nightingale has a parrot today, a great feature of the residents' lounge.

The gardens were well maintained, and enjoyed by the residents in the summer. They were also allowed to make short trips outside the Home during the day, but only within certain hours. The residents could receive visits, but again only during very limited hours in the afternoons; Saturdays and most Jewish festivals were excluded. This made it very difficult for relatives living in the East End, who normally worked a six day week, to visit their family member, and for some it would have been nearly impossible. To reach the Home those travelling from the East End could take the City and South London Electric Railway from the Bank, and then go by the halfpenny London County Council tram to the corner of Nightingale Lane. Those travelling from the West End took a train from Victoria to Wandsworth Common Station. Visiting hours remained essentially unchanged for many years.

While this might sound uninviting by modern standards, by the standards of its time they were advanced, especially when compared to the workhouse or destitution on the streets. Residents received good medical attention and diet, and had regular treats and excursions. Contemporary documentary evidence confirms that the regime was administered in a liberal and caring fashion, though there were regularly reports of residents who left because they could not adapt to the ethos of the Home.

The 1910 rules are vivid and informative, and when reading them it is worth bearing in mind that most rules and regulations are not developed in a vacuum but are based on particular problems and misdemeanours that have occurred.

RULES AND REGULATIONS 1910

1. *Inmates are not allowed on admission to bring anything with them except clean clothing.*

2. *All inmates are subject to the authority of the Master and Matrons whose instructions must be strictly obeyed.*

3. *The inmates shall be required to perform such duties as the Master and Matrons may direct. Exemption from the performance of such duties will only be granted on the certificate of the Medical Officer or by permission of the Chairman of the House Committee.*

4. *Divine service must be attended by all male inmates. On Sabbaths and Festivals no inmate may be absent from Synagogue service except with the permission of the Master or Matron.*

5. *Inmates may absent themselves from the Home between the hours of 10 & 12 and 2 & 6 if presentably attired but AT NO OTHER TIME except by permission of the Master. Infringements of the rule will render the offender liable to expulsion from the Home.*

6. *Quarrelling and the use of unseemly language are strictly prohibited.*

7. *Inmates are not allowed to bring food into the Institution except with approval of the Master or Matron. Food brought into the Home without such approval will be confiscated.*

8. *No medicines may be procured or used except by sanction of the Medical Officer.*

9. *Inmates may receive Visitors on Sundays, Tuesdays and Thursdays between the hours of 2 & 6 in Summer and 2 & 5 in Winter. Visitors are not allowed in the dining-hall during meal-time.*

10. *Smoking is allowed only in the men's sitting room and the garden. Spitting is strictly prohibited.*

11. *Inmates are not allowed to engage in business or undertake any employment outside the Home.*

A flavour of what life was like in the Home can be gleaned from the Committee minutes and the annual reports. The minutes provide us with 'snap-shots' of the day to day conditions and incidents in the Home. One strong impression is that to keep costs down the Home was always seeking the lowest tenders for goods and services. The subject of food was frequently raised in the context of economy. On one occasion it was resolved to ask the House Committee if they could substitute some meat meals with fish to save on money and to ask the advice of the medical officer on the question. On another occasion the Master was instructed to keep the consumption of beer by the Stewards to the lowest possible minimum, and expenditure on this was not to exceed eight shillings per month. Beer remained a staple of the working person's daily diet until early in the twentieth century and drinking during working hours was the norm, so this was quite a harsh restriction.

In 1910, the Home employed a total of 25 staff; they were listed as 15 domestic servants, 2 stokers, 1 laundry aid, 2 handymen, 1 cook, 1 master and 2 matrons, 1 gardener. The wage bill totalled £1189 a year.

The relationship between the Master and the Committee was not that of equals, but of employee and employer. The Committee had the final say on the running of the Home and expected the Master to enact their decisions. This is illustrated by an incident of 1910 when the Committee went ahead with ordering matzahs from Leeds, despite the Master's report that the residents would not be able to eat them, presumably on the grounds of indigestibility.

The selection of inmates was, of course, a vital element in the administration of the Home. The Investigating Committee under-took the task of assessing likely cases and reported back to the General Committee with their recommendations. By 1914 this was a well-established routine that involved members of the Committee making home inquiries in the East End, and the Visiting Medical Officer carrying out medical examinations.

Detailed records of the selection process can be found in the Minute Book. While there is no evidence of a formal set of acceptance or rejection criteria, a general pattern can be observed. The initial question was whether the applicant was in real need and if he or she was genuinely past work. Applicants had to be in very difficult straits, if not dire straits, before they could be made a priority case. They would also usually be in a poor physical condition, often malnourished. Other than this, respectability was the key issue, and how well they were spoken of by referees or in

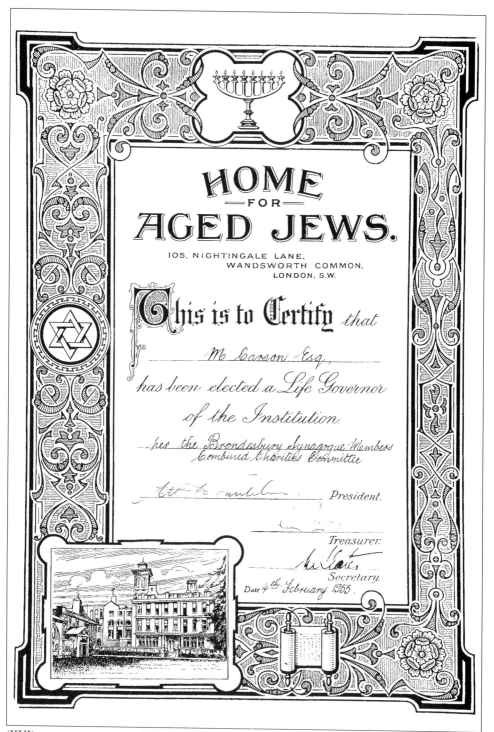

HOME
FOR
AGED JEWS.

105, NIGHTINGALE LANE,
WANDSWORTH COMMON,
LONDON, S.W.

This is to Certify that

M. Carson Esq,

has been elected a Life Governor

of the Institution.

per the Brondesbury Synagogue Members
Combined Charities Committee

_____ President.

Treasurer.

Secretary.

Date 4th February 1953.

(XVI)   *Certificate presented to Life Governors.*

(XVII)   *An outing to Westcliff-on-Sea, 1953.*

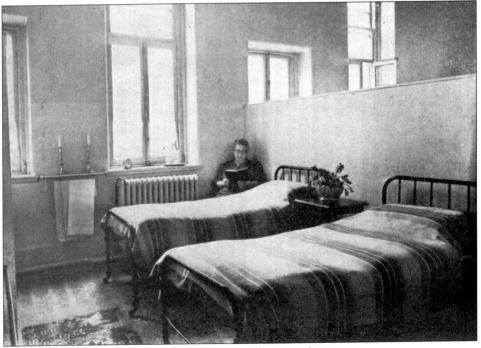

(XVIII)   *A cubicle in one of the wards.*

(XIX)

The occupational therapy room in the 1950s.

(XX)   *Princess Diana at the Home, 1983. 'She's an ace' said the card players.*
                                                                    [Peter Fisher]

(XXI)   *The Duke of Edinburgh at the opening of Birchlands in 1980.*   *[Peter Fisher]*

(XXII)   *Gerald Lipton, Vivien Duffield and Cecil Elsom at the David Clore Memorial Fund Dinner, 1985.*

(XXIII) *David Clore and the Duke of Marlborough at the Blenheim Palace dinner, 1984.*
[Peter Fisher]

(XXIV) *Barnett Shine, Lord Jakobovits, Sir Charles Clore and Sir Michael Sobell at the*
opening of the Red Brick Extension.   *[Peter Fisher]*

(XXV)   Visitor Sir Yehudi Menuhin, resident Louba Rubin, Asher Corren and Lord Rayne, 1992.   [Peter Fisher]

(XXVI)   *Ernest L. Franklin.*
President 1899–1933.

(XXVII)   *Sir Charles Abrahams.*
President 1970–1973.

(XXVIII)   *Alfred Cope.*
President 1955–1967.

(XXIX)   *Cecil Elsom.*
President 1973–1993.

the community. Candidates were favoured if they had been hard working and honest and fallen on hard times through no fault of their own. Cleanliness of their person and accommodation was also an important consideration. A record of regular Jewish religious observance and charitable giving and involvement were always a major additional recommendation to the selectors. All applicants who were former subscribers were admitted, including one of the founders of the Jewish Workhouse.

Those who were rejected were turned down either because they were not considered in sufficient need, or could still work, or were the author of their own misfortunes. Bad references, poor character, and uncleanliness, were the other principal grounds. One man was rejected mainly because he had been stated to have treated his wife very badly. Religious grounds for rejection were lack of Jewish observance, and worst of all leaving the Jewish fold. One applicant, Daniel de Fries, was rejected because he had married a Christian, as had two of their five children.

The reports are of considerable social significance and reveal in some detail what poverty of the Jewish aged was like at the turn of the twentieth century. Applicants are variously described as being, 'found in almost starving conditions', 'living on crusts of bread', 'suffering from privation and exposure', 'nearly penniless and known to the soup kitchen', 'in the workhouse', 'in great distress having pawned all their belongings'.

Some applicants were surviving only because they were being helped by old friends or associates, or by a kindly landlady. Others found informal help from their congregation, or by sharing rooms with another elderly person. The Jewish Board of Guardians often provided a small weekly sum or attempted to get a business restarted with a small grant.

Many applicants had fallen in need either because they had no children or because their children were too poor to help them. Some children lived abroad, or simply did not want to help their parents due to family problems.

The following examples, taken from an official report of 24 October 1905, are typical. There were thirteen vacancies at the time, seven for women and six for men. Frederick S. Franklin was chairman of the Committee:

LEWIS B. 83, Park Lane. Age 73. In England forty years. First application. Widower, has two daughters, living with one who is not able to keep him any longer; the other daughter formerly gave him a weekly allowance but cannot now afford to continue same. Applicant appears very respectable and is recommended for admission.

MICHAEL D. 4, Mackay Buildings, Curtain Road. Age 80. English born. First application. Single. Applicant was a Showman but is now past work. Has no means, but gets a little help from his nephews who are poor. Kept his mother for forty years. Has lived at present address fifteen years. Was urged by relations to apply some time ago but refused, but now forced to do so having no other resource. A very respectable old man and recommended for admission.

ADELAIDE F. 63, Eric Street, Mile End. Age 60. In England ten years. First application. Lives with a daughter who has seven children (one married), who does not appear to be in good circumstances. Is not an undeserving case, but in view of the age and present circumstances of applicant, is not recommended.

JACOB J. 16, Hessel Street, Commercial Road. Age 64. First application. In England ten years. Widower. Has two sons and lives with one of them. Does not appear to be past work and is not recommended.

REBECCA L. 64, Ernest Street, Stepney. Age 75. In England nine years. Third application. Was formerly not considered pressing in view of better cases, but is now recommended for admission.

FRANCES L. 25, Princes Square, St. Georges. Age 72. English born. First application. Widow. Has four sons from whom she gets very little help. Gets 6/- weekly from the Board, and 5/- weekly from a private source. Has very good character from references and appears very respectable. Recommended for admission.

ISAAC L. Rowton House, Newington Butts. Age 61. In England forty-six years. First application. Single. Unable to work owing to defective eyesight and weakness. Only relations are two sisters who are poor; is suffering from privation and exposure. Very respectable and recommended for admission.

FELIX S. 15, Well Street, Cable Street. Age 64. In England forty-six years. First application. Wife died recently and he is stated to have treated her badly, character is also otherwise unsatisfactory and he is not recommended.

HANNAH T. 9–11, Fouberts Place, Regent Street. Age 70. In England thirteen years. First application. Has a daughter who appears able to support her. Not recommended.

FANNY Z. 14, Palmer Street, Spitalfields. Age 67. In England forty-two years. First application. Been a Widow twenty years, is in great poverty, and has pawned her belongings. Has three sons unable to help. Appears very clean and respectable, and is recommended for admission.

GEORGE P. Newington Workhouse. Age 77; WOOLF F. South Grove Union, E. Age 69; HYAM E. Medway Union, Chatham. Age 85. Unsatisfactory characters and not recommended.

Three further paying cases were presented – one was withdrawn, and two were disqualified by the Medical Officer. There were seven other ordinary cases, one of whom had since died, three were disqualified by the Medical Officer, and the remainder failed to attend the Medical examinations or to present themselves before the Committee.

Discipline was maintained in a reasonably relaxed manner. Residents who infringed the more important rules were reported to the House Committee. For the most part they received a ticking off and a formal caution for anti-social activities such as possessing another inmate's belongings or for being very quarrelsome. The problem was speedily dealt with, and that was the end of the matter. Those who continued to offend, or who were guilty of violent behaviour, were referred to the General Committee who had the ultimate power of expulsion, but this was very rarely enforced.

One sad and difficult case concerned a Miss Van Raalte who suffered regular nervous attacks that were inconvenient to the other inmates. The Committee debated whether they could remove her, but found that they could not as she was not judged insane by the Doctor.

Residents sometimes became disenchanted with the Home or could not adapt and felt obliged to leave surreptitiously. In one case two residents absconded the Home, one removing her belongings by stealth. In 1910, a Mr. Morris Goldman (aged 72 in 1909), of 7 Cur Street, Nottingham had been in the Home for eighteen months. He announced to the Committee that he had decided to leave as the climate in London did not agree with him and he could earn his own living. The Committee were angry when he admitted that he had a house and furniture back in Nottingham, and that he had taken advantage of the benefits of the charity.

Most residents were extremely happy with their lot. The son of one elderly man, who had passed away, wrote in 1915, 'His closing years were spent in peace and happiness in the Home. In fact, he has often told me that the seventeen years he spent there were the happiest period of his life. The Master and Matrons, I know, did everything in their power to make him comfortable'. Such sentiments were expressed across the decades, and perhaps best typify the true character of the Charity.

XI

THE CHANGING OF THE GUARD
1900–1914

Between 1900 and 1914 the Home suffered considerable physical and emotional upheaval. This was due to the move to Nightingale Lane, and the fact that most of its key members and founders passed away in the period that the Home was undergoing its greatest development.

S. A. Green died in 1899, and F. D. Mocatta in 1905. Thus the founder and the saviour of the Jewish Workhouse died within a few short years of each other, after over thirty years service to the organisation. The grief-stricken committee concluded their eulogy of Mocatta by recalling that, 'His sympathy with the old folks was unbounded, and when in town he regularly visited the Homes, where his genial presence, and his charming and affable demeanour were a source of joy and happiness to the inmates'.

Barrow Emanuel died in 1904, having been Vice President for twenty years until his retirement in 1899, and having served the Homes for nearly twenty-five years. An able deputy to Mocatta, he was a man of considerable tact and discretion, and played a most valuable role on the Building Committee.

The loss of Lewis Levy in 1913 was a particular blow as he was a Committee member of the Hand in Hand from 1880, and was one of the original delegates appointed to amalgamate the Hand in Hand with the Widows' Home. He was also Honorary Auditor for the Home.

Isaac Samuel's demise in 1914 caused great sadness, since without his efforts *Ferndale* and Lord Wandsworth's benefaction might never have been secured. Henry L. Harris passed away in the same year. He was President of the Widows' Home for many years prior to the amalgamation with the Hand in Hand in 1885, and an active committee member in the Home for Aged Jews, completing over fifty years' service for the Homes.

While a listing of the great and dead of the charities may seem maudlin, it illustrates the remarkable talents and dedication that the Homes attracted over the years. With the challenges that the Great War and the Depression were to deliver, it is a testimony to the commitment of the newer committee members that they were able to direct the charity through some very troubled times.

XII

WORLD WAR I AND NIGHTINGALE
1914–1918

World War I conditions set a grave challenge to the Home, one that threatened its very existence, but it was to be a challenge that was merely a minor rehearsal for the depression years that were to follow. The Home was to learn that the stable prices of decades, and indeed centuries, had ended, and that inflation was to remain a regular, if not constant, feature throughout the twentieth century.

General difficulties in the national economy not only reduced the Home's income from subscriptions as economic problems bit into donors' incomes, but greatly increased the call upon their services. Many elderly East End Jews suddenly found that the line between just coping and being in serious difficulties had been crossed, and applications to the Home increased. Many subscribers who passed away were not replaced by newer recruits. Squaring the circle between less income and greater demand was to be a long-term recurrent problem.

During the War commodity prices almost doubled, the cost of food soared, and staff costs increased by forty per cent. In 1913, the Home's expenditure was £3,753; in 1919 £6,378.

Compensatory sources of income, or savings, had to be found. The Aid Societies produced sterling performances and increased their income. The three branches of the Aid Society merged in 1916 to improve their effectiveness. Jewish Friendly Societies, such as Achei Brith and Shield of Abraham made donations, Mr Cash playing a particularly important role in realising these. Local cinemas donated part of their takings from Sunday performances. The usual fundraising activities proved profitable; a bazaar organised by Moss Harris in 1914 was a great success, raising £472.

A financial benefit was gained because the Home 'dug for victory' in response to the war time call. Fortunately, the vegetable garden had been enlarged in 1913 and the greenhouse rebuilt, and it was reported with evident satisfaction that the residents were being fed on increasing amounts of home-grown vegetables. At the end of the War the Medical Officer concluded that the restricted diet (and no doubt the organic vegetables) had been beneficial to the residents' health and he could see no reason to alter it.

The Home was also helped by the fact that it was still in relatively newly refurbished premises with low maintenance costs, and its capital had been supplemented in 1907 by the sale of the original Stepney Green premises for £2,750.

Despite every effort, the Home's annual deficit rose to £1,000 in 1916. Though the situation had improved by 1918, reducing to £277, by 1920 it was back up to £1,006.

Some of the staff were called up for war service, leading to a staff shortage. The most notable absentee was the Secretary, Mr Maurice Myers. The War increased opportunities for the advancement of women. Floie Kelf, who had been appointed Assistant Secretary to Myers, took over his work once he had departed for France. At the end of the War Myers resigned and Kelf took over as Secretary, an influential post she held to the end of World War II.

Despite the difficulties, the Home continued to make commendable efforts to improve care and service for the residents. In 1913, an ophthalmologist was appointed. Mr A. H. Levy FRCS became Honorary Ophthalmic Surgeon and visited the Home regularly. It was the first of a number of ancillary services that were to follow.

A change in the Home's role was now becoming apparent. It was increasingly being seen not just in terms of a place to spend one's declining years and escape destitution. It was becoming appreciated that there was much still to be gained and enjoyed in the closing years of life. Mr Van Leer, the Honorary Secretary of the Aid Society, acted as an informal entertainments officer. He arranged a much appreciated regular programme of events, principally concerts during the winter months, that brought 'brightness and pleasure into the lives of the inmates'.

While the storms of war largely failed to interrupt the peace of the Home, its end was followed by the visit of the 1920 influenza epidemic which killed more of the population of Europe than World War I. The epidemic took hold in the Home – the first it had ever experienced – and killed ten residents before it passed. Both Matrons became ill with the virus, and extra nursing help had to be called in. Considering the virulence of the epidemic the casualties were remarkably few, due to the excellent nursing care provided at the Home.

XIII

THE DEPRESSION AND INTER-WAR YEARS 1918–1939

The ending of World War I did not bring an end to the Home's difficulties; on the contrary it proved to be the prelude to three decades of fresh problems. The years of trade depression that followed the War, and World War II itself, were years of crisis. Despite this, the Home continued to develop and evolve.

By 1922, national economic problems began to affect Nightingale, peaking, so far as it was concerned, in 1931. During this period Nightingale sustained a serious loss of income and accumulated an almost overwhelming deficit of £7,000, and had to fight to stay open.

As before, as trade decreased so the number of applicants increased. In 1922, the number of beds had to be increased to 155 to cope with the extra demand. Additional space was released by rearranging the wards. Demand became such that by 1924 the Home had to abandon its policy of admitting only once every three or four months. Instead it admitted on a continuing basis as vacancies arose.

Things worsened in 1931. By then many older people who had been securely supported by their own families found that the families could no longer help. This led to a fresh crop of applicants for admission to the Home, including many of its long-term subscribers and supporters who were now themselves in difficulties. The problem was compounded in 1932. Many residents already in the Home were supported by relatives who paid maintenance. Times were so hard that these families could no longer continue their contributions, and the Home had to accept the *fait accompli* and tear up the financial agreements they had made, and take over the cost.

An emergency appeal made jointly with the Home of Rest through an advertisement in the *Jewish Chronicle* brought in a welcome £4,400.

In 1932–3 the Home was bursting at the seams, with cramped conditions in the wards and rooms. Such was the pressure that in 1932 the Home arranged for applicants who had been accepted for entry, but who were waiting for a vacancy to arise, to stay at the Jews' Temporary Shelter in Leman Street until a bed became available.

During this disquieting period it was very much a matter of all hands to the pumps – economies had to be achieved, and new money found. Helena de Niet, the Matron, saved £108 in nursing costs, and Mrs Rege Breuer, the Housekeeper, also made savings in her department. Another strategy, initiated in World War I, was now expanded. The Home encouraged the direct donations of goods, many of which were supplied by the Aid Societies. The reasoning was that a purchase saved was money saved.

The time had come when drastic steps had to be taken, and a Special Economy Committee was appointed. When it reported back its major recommendation, made reluctantly, was that the Home should scale back on staff and residents. A reduction was made of thirty residents and three staff. Another key saving was effected by persuading the adjacent Home of Rest to take over the financial responsibility for twenty-five beds that had until then been at the charge of the Home.

The Sunday cinema screenings that had been a major source of income worth around £1,000 each year, were reduced by half in 1932 following a change in the law. Once again, the Aid Societies came to the rescue and increased their collections.

Some new income came from a medley of sources – Jewish clubs, guilds and societies. These were often small sums, but they all added up and were appreciated.

A great success story of the time was the Ezra Society founded in 1931 by David Cope at the Brixton Synagogue in Effra Road. Cope was evidently a man of uncommon fundraising ability, and in its first six months the Society raised £500; in 1933 £1,357. It continued to raise substantial sums, and the Cope name was to be closely linked with the continuing history of the Home.

State welfare legislation began to affect the development of the Home, for the better. From early in the twentieth century governments started, little by little, to create a pension system that gradually ameliorated and eventually replaced the Poor Law and the workhouse. In its early years the system excluded many Jews – those who did not meet the residency requirements, and those who were self-employed. By 1930, however, pension income became important to the Home as more East End Jews became eligible to receive the benefit. In 1931, income from residents' pensions was £1,524. The Home was also able to increase contributions made by relatives of residents who could now afford it, a source that brought in £1,021 in the same year. The government introduced a tax rebate for donations made to charities under a deed of covenant, and the Committee seized upon this as a means of increasing income, though covenants were not taken up as widely as the Home had hoped. The state increasingly, directly and indirectly, helped fund the running of the Home.

The Home always zealously fought to maintain its independence. For this reason it resisted attempts made in 1925 to persuade it to affiliate to the Central Council of Jewish Charities, and in 1930 applied successfully to be exempted from the provisions of the Nurses' Home Registration Act.

By the start of the 1920s, the facilities and buildings were beginning to show their age. The laundry was expanded in 1921, central heating extended to the Davis and Franklin Wings in 1922, and a new heating system installed in 1927 at the great cost of £4,000.

The majority of the staff lived on site, the nurses particularly, but their accommodation was by now substandard. In 1927, five nurses were living in temporary accommodation in unhealthy, damp rooms above the garages at the rear of the Home. That year an extension to the Nurses' Home was completed at a cost of £1,452, and that helped to alleviate the problem. The cost of this new wing and of a new heating system was partly met in the following year by the sale of the freehold of the old Hackney Home for £3,500.

The quarters for the twenty-five domestic staff were also of very poor quality, being the loft area at the top of the house. They had been condemned as unsafe in World War I and had to be replaced. Renovations were made to the façade, and the dangerous central tower removed – though one suspects it had long been a redundant feature as the view from the top could rarely have been sought by the residents.

Mr Van Leer continued arranging his regular entertainments. He celebrated his sixty-fifth birthday in 1925 and the Home and residents made him a presentation. He died in 1927. Modern technology reached the Home with the addition of a wireless set in 1925. Many residents also became regular visitors to the Balham Picture House. A telephone was installed in 1927 ('Battersea 1536').

Despite all difficulties, the Home continued to make commendable efforts to improve conditions. The existing eye care arrangements continued to be developed, and in-house ear and dental care were introduced in 1923–4. One important area that had to be addressed was the lack of provision for infirm candidates. In 1923 there was just one small ward and a few nursing staff, barely sufficient for existing inmates who became temporarily ill or became infirm after admission. Because of this, there simply was no accommodation for those *arriving* infirm and one fifth of all new applicants had to be turned away on medical grounds.

This concerned the Home, particularly the Medical Officer, as too many of its residents who were ill were already having to be sent out of the Home to Poor Law infirmaries or other institutions solely for the reason that they were too old and feeble to look after themselves. The Committee appealed to the Jewish public:

> The community will appreciate that these infirm cases are often the most deserving that come before the Committee, who, if they had adequate facilities to do so, would admit them at once. Many of these unfortunate applicants are at present living in poor and overcrowded homes and become a burden not only to themselves but to their kindred. The Committee feel sure that an appeal to the community for funds to meet this claim will result in a ready response. Down through the ages and all over the world the Jew has been known to mankind as the protector and supporter of his aged: surely there is a double claim upon him from those who are not only aged but also infirm.

So the Home increased its provision with extra beds for the infirm within the Home. The greatest shortage was for beds for infirm women; to overcome this a general ward was converted for the purpose. A further ward was provided for the chronically infirm.

This was a highly significant step, as it marked the embryonic stage of a developing policy enabling residents to stay in the care of the Home even after they became ill or infirm. This also set the precedent for a continuing drive over the next decades to provide increased facilities for such residents.

Later twenty beds were obtained for the chronically infirm in a ward at the adjacent Jewish Home of Rest.

In 1930, the Home opened two new single rooms for the severely ill or dying, a development that was considered important for the dignity of those residents who were at the stage that they needed privacy.

That most modern of geriatric problems, provision for those with age-related psychiatric problems, became a live point of discussion more than ninety years ago.

There was a growth in the number of inmates suffering from psychiatric illness, probably linked to residents' increasing age of entry which during World War I had risen to eighty. The average length of stay was then seven years. This difficult issue was tackled in 1930. As a first step it was decided to admit all new residents on one month's probation, in case they proved to be unsuitable for retention because of such illness.

Ernest Franklin, who was born in 1859, retired from the Presidency in 1933 after almost thirty-five years in the office. Donald Van den Bergh J.P. succeeded him. Franklin had been in great measure responsible for the growth of the Home and for the successful amalgamation. He paid close attention to every detail of the internal management, and continued as a Vice President. He was still attending meetings at the age of ninety. He died in April 1950

By 1935, the Committee fully appreciated that, once again, its existing facilities were becoming dated, and declared that 'the time has come for the remodelling of the building on modern lines so that the community may possess in the Home a building of which it can be truly proud and which may serve as a symbol of the loving care and attention bestowed by Jewry on its aged and infirm'.

New plans were made. In 1937 the Home was rewired, and in 1938 extensive new sanitation installed. An additional ward for the infirm was opened on 11 February 1937, and a new nurses' wing was planned in 1937 at a cost of £3,000. The old accommodation was knocked down in 1939 in preparation for this redevelopment, but that work was cancelled at the outset of the War.

In addition to applications from those who had long been resident in England, many hundreds were now being received from Germany on behalf of elderly and destitute refugees who would face starvation unless taken charge of under the guarantee of a communal organisation in England. The Committee decided to house as many German nationals as accommodation would permit. The maintenance of those admitted was borne by the German Jewish Aid Committee; the cost of the additional equipment needed was defrayed privately by members of the Committee.

The Home was evolving a more professional philosophy of care for the older person. In 1938, the term 'social well being' was mentioned for the first time as an issue in care. If World War II had not intervened, the Home would almost certainly have modernised both its practice and buildings at the end of the 1930s. The War compelled all such plans to be put to one side, and the Home was forced to defend its very existence against a lack of money, shortages, and Nazi bombs.

XIV

WORLD WAR II

In 1937, the residents of Nightingale quietly celebrated the coronation of George VI. Unaware of the storms that were brewing, they were taken on a drive round the coronation route to see the decorations, and a special synagogue service was held at the Home.

The impending threat to the calm pattern of everyday life was evident when an air raid shelter was installed in 1938. It transpired that the shelter would be rarely used despite the air raids of 1941–2.

As war approached the Committee seriously considered evacuating the Home to the country, but found there was a total lack of suitable and convenient premises. Emergency stocks of food were built up for the 170 residents and 40 staff. Once the war started, it was not very long before many of the younger staff went on active service. Colonel Van den Berg, the President of the Home, was sent on diplomatic service to North Africa.

Diminishing income meant that the Home soon had to make further reductions in staff and residents. No new cases were admitted in 1940, and the resident roll fell to 142 in 1941, to 132 in 1942, and to 121 in 1944.

In June 1944, the neighbouring Jewish Home of Rest was directly hit by a flying bomb and a number of nurses were killed. Nightingale suffered extensive blast damage but little structural damage – only the laundry was demolished. The staff managed to dig the laundry machine out and salvage it.

There were no fatalities at Nightingale, but the assistant matron, Miss A. H. Foster, was tragically killed in her home during the night when getting dressed in readiness to respond to the raid. By the time her relatives received the body from the authorities none of her personal effects could be found. Looting of the dead was a common, but unreported curse of the Blitz.

Due to the blast damage, the residents were all evacuated to LCC hospitals and rest centres where they stayed for four and a half months. Fifty women were accommodated in the Myrdle Street Rest Centre in Stepney, East London, greatly helped by Miriam Moses who made their welfare her special concern. The administration of the Home was carried on in temporary offices in the City until the staff and residents could return to the patched up Home. The Medical Officer was pleasantly surprised to see how well the residents had coped with these dramatic events and had suffered no apparent ill effects.

For the senior female staff who carried most of the burden of running the Home during the War, it was a different story. The stress of the raids and bombing adversely affected the Matron and Housekeeper, Mrs Niet and Mrs Breuer, who both retired in 1944 on health grounds. Mrs Kelf-Cohen, who retired immediately at the end of the war, suffered from heart disease probably caused by stress. Impelled by her sense of duty she went to the Home even during air raids, and was forced on more than one occasion to complete her bus journey crouched under a seat as the bombs were exploding around her.

All the staff, drastically reduced in numbers due to other war duties, worked extremely hard and with great dedication, each of them doing the work of several. In 1944 the Home was dismayed when Colonel Van Den Berg retired on personal grounds.

Financial matters were a major issue. There was a sharp drop in income at the start of the War, as much personal and communal giving was directed towards supporting refugees from Germany. As in World War I, the Home experienced the same pattern of rising expenditure as commodity prices and wages rose sharply. Wages increased steeply, partly due to inflationary pressures and partly because the Home adopted agreed national pay scales. For nurses, the Home followed scales set out in the Rushcliffe Report on Nurses' Salaries, and for the domestic staff they abided by the Whitley Council Scale. General expenditure was double that of pre-War.

Fortunately, the Home's intense efforts in the previous two decades to extend its sources of income had borne fruit and improved its financial stability. Nevertheless, the Home was compelled to dip into its cash reserves in 1939, and by 1940 was taking money from legacies to plug financial gaps.

In 1942, Nightingale, seeking to repeat its earlier success, inserted an advertisement in the *Jewish Chronicle*, hoping to raise 3,000 Guineas. Hopes were dashed; only 300 guineas was received.

As the Allied Forces advanced across Europe and the end of the War appeared to be in sight, the plans for new buildings and improvements that had been put on hold were taken out and were being aired again, and the number of residents was gradually increased.

As in the past, the income from the Aid Societies was important, and a new society formed in 1945 in Brighton and Hove became a significant contributor immediately post War.

Subscriptions remained weak, and counted for only a very small proportion of overall income. Despite this, the Home stood steadfastly by its long held conviction that such a source ought to be developed, and many annual reports decried the public's neglect in this area. In reality, subscriptions had ceased to be of importance from the end of the Victorian era.

Active discussions took place about moving to an entirely new site. Difficult matters of judgement were involved. To stay put and develop the existing site was one option, but the size of the site was clearly a potentially limiting factor. The question of location was discussed in depth. Most of London's Jewish population had left the East End and dispersed to the north and north-west of London, to the promised land of Golders Green and its environs. Some felt that not to move would be an opportunity lost. The arguments were delicately balanced, but as no suitable site was found the decision was made to stay where they were. This was in many senses a crucial decision for the Home, one that has shaped its entire development in the past fifty years.

The plan adopted at the end of the War aimed to provide a 'truly Jewish Home' in a brand new building, built to a high specification. The Committee urged upon the Jewish community: 'For those who have passed safely through the perils of the war there is no better way of expressing thanks to Providence than by sending a thanksgiving offering to the Home'. Post-war restrictions on new buildings delayed the start of work for several years. In the meantime the Home was refurbished and the gardens laid out again.

A far-reaching innovation was the establishment, in 1949, of an Occupational Therapy department, provided in line with the latest thinking on care for the older person. The department, initially situated in a prefab hut, made a slow start but came to revolutionise the conditions in the Home for many residents, and heralded many new departures in care that make the Home what it is today.

XV

WOMEN AND NIGHTINGALE

Charity work was one of the few areas in which, in the nineteenth century, Jewish women from respectable families were able to hold responsible positions in the practical running of institutions. At Nightingale there were many middle and upper class women who could be counted amongst those who helped create a modern, independent role for women.

They took a significant part in the running of the Home, both at a practical level and also, from the early twentieth century, at committee level too. It is to the credit of the forward thinking of the Home that by the 1930s half the committee posts were occupied by women.

Though it took some time for women to attain senior posts on the committees, they wielded much influence elsewhere. The Matrons were extremely influential as for many years, after the departure of the last Master of the Home in the 1920s, they ran not just the nursing staff and the nursing care of the Home, but were also responsible for many other areas of management. On the administration side, the appointment of Floie Kelf-Cohen as Secretary after the First World War was very significant. She exercised considerable influence over the years and, as has been seen, ran the Home during World War II when so many of the staff were absent.

Sarah Magnus, who died in 1874 aged seventy-four, was Matron of the Hand in Hand Asylum for many years. She was the daughter-in-law of Simon Magnus, a rich merchant, one of the leaders of the Chatham community, Mayor of Queenborough, and a man of good works. Chatham Memorial Synagogue was built in his memory after he died tragically from an overdose of chloroform taken to allay the toothache.

Sarah's early presence at the Hand in Hand made her a pioneer for women in her class, and may compare in that role with Elizabeth H. Levi who worked at Charcroft House in the East End for twenty-five years, and Alice Model the dominant figure in the East End for providing nursing assistance to sick or pregnant women, both of whom came from middle class families.

The link to Chatham helps explain the support the Hand in Hand had from leading Jewish Chatham families, the Isaacs, the Pykes and the Castellos. Lizzie Magnus married one of the Castellos of Jews' Walk, Sydenham Hill. The Castellos were a leading Sephardi family, and its members included senior officials at Bevis Marks Synagogue and generous supporters of Beth Holim. In the 1870s they gave large subscriptions to the Hand in Hand.

Sara Magnus (d. 1927), a family relative of Sarah Magnus, was the first female member of the General Committee, and first Chair of a Ladies' Committee of the Home. She followed a long family tradition of service, which was perhaps the reason for her elevation to the committees.

Ellen Levy, (born c.1849), the wife of Angel Levy a litho printer, had a remarkable and lengthy career as Matron, serving during each amalgamation of the three charities. She was the Matron of the Widows' Home in Prescott Street from 1878, of the Well Street branch of the Widows' Home, of the combined Widows' Home and Hand in Hand Asylum in Well Street until 1907, and at Nightingale Lane where she became Joint Matron of the Home for Aged Jews with Mrs Van Molen.

Ellen completed forty-five years of service in 1922. During her final year Katie Harris took over the most onerous of her duties, and Ellen was semi-retired in post. Mr. Harry Harris recalls 'I can remember being taken to the Home in 1927 when I was about four years old and being introduced to a very dignified lady with a starched high collar who I had to call Aunt Ellen. I think I was a bit scared of her'. The Home still has in its possession the large inscribed silver tray presented to her in 1907.

Little is known about Katie Van Molen and her husband Lou Van Molen who in the late 1890s became the first Master of Nightingale House, other than that they were of Dutch origin. There was a distinct Dutch tradition of service in the Home, possibly explained

69

by the fact that the Dutch had a reputation for their cleanliness and excellence in all things domestic.

Mrs Van Molen died in 1922 after a distressing illness, shortly after her silver Wedding. Katie Harris, who had been appointed assistant Matron in 1920, was promoted to Matron following Mrs. van Molen's death. Katie evidently became close to the very much older Lou van Molen and they married only a year after Mrs Van Molen's passing. Katie was an engaging character. As an independent eighteen-year-old, she showed interest in the Zionist movement and visited Palestine. There she contracted a liver disease that was eventually to claim her life at the age of sixty. After she left the Home, and after the death of Lou, she founded her own old people's home at Clapton in 1937.

Mrs. Eve, who retired thorough ill health in 1930, Mrs Rege Breuer, (appointed 1928), and Helena de Niet (appointed 1931) were all highly regarded matrons who enjoyed the love and respect of the residents.

Floie Kelf-Cohen (1889–1964), was an independent, talented, and modern woman well ahead of her times. Her mother was Dutch, and her brother fought in the Boer War. As we have seen, she took over as Secretary at the end of World War I. During World War II she had the 'great, almost single-handed, responsibility' of running the Home. Her sphere of influence widened in 1926 when, following the departure of Mr Van Molen, the post of Master was never filled again. Her husband, Reuben Cohen, who served as an officer in World War I and was a brilliant scholar at Wadham College, Oxford said that her devotion to the Home was the principal interest in her life, and her daughter, Judy Kelly, remembers that her work took precedence over family life, though that was never neglected. She was more interested in geriatrics than paediatrics. During World War II she rescued many Jewish refugee girls under the pretext of using them as au pairs, one of whom was informally adopted by her. She had widespread interests. She was a founder member of the South London Liberal Synagogue at Streatham, and was actively and devotedly involved with another old age home, the Maude Nathan Home. She was also an accomplished self-taught artist; her illuminated copy of the Book of Kells was on display for some years in the Trinity College library and is in its own way a small masterpiece. She was well ahead of her times, and many modern women would identify with her style of life. It is a credit to Nightingale that it could attract and keep the services of so remarkable a woman.

Ida Hyman (d. 1979), a daughter of Moss Harris, had a sixty year association with the Home. She was chairman of the Ladies' Committee before 1949 and later became a member of the Executive Committee and a Vice-President of the Home. She was associated with Nightingale for over sixty years.

Anne Stern, the wife of Maxwell Stern, was Chairman of Nightingale from 1977 to 1985, and is referred to again in the following chapter on the Levy family.

Miriam Moses O.B.E. (1885–1965), the Mayor of Stepney in 1931, is one of the most celebrated women to have been associated with Nightingale. The daughter of a magistrate, from a young age she involved herself in Jewish communal matters. She was the founder of the Brady Girls' Club, served on the Board of Deputies, and campaigned for Jewish women's causes. She had a significant involvement with Nightingale that started when she helped the Home in her capacity as Committee member for the Home of Rest in 1925. She went on to serve on the Committee of Nightingale itself, and was a very active and able member.

XVI

SIX GENERATIONS OF SERVICE –
THE LEVY FAMILY

The Levy Family and their descendants occupy a remarkable niche in the history of the Home, and perhaps even in the annals of Anglo-Jewish charity work. The family can claim over 150 years and six generations of unbroken service.

It all started with Lawrence Levy (1828–1890), who was a founder of the Widows' Home when it was in Prescott Street (not the original foundation of the charity itself) and worked for the Home from the 1850s.

George Cohen (1828–1890), married Lawrence Levy's sister Amelia, and was President of the Hand in Hand and the Widows' Home.

Lewis Levy (1847–1913), the eldest son of Lawrence Levy, carried on his father's good work by acting as Honorary Auditor of the Widows' Home. He also served as Overseer of the Poor for the United Synagogue, and in 1890 was a joint founder, with the Rev Joseph Stern, of the Orphan Aid Society. He served on the Committees of the Home for Aged Jews, the Jews' Orphan Asylum, and the Jews' Free School.

Percy Levy was the son of Lewis Levy, and in 1912 he founded a charity for the benefit of the Home that he named the 'Percy Levy Collection'. He was helped in this work by his brother George – they had started collecting as children. The Percy Levy Collection merged with the North West London Aid Society in 1919. Over the years this Aid Society has succeeded in raising millions of pounds for Nightingale.

Percy was Joint Treasurer of the Home for many years until his death in January 1964. In 1962 he was presented with a silver salver to commemorate his fifty years service to the Home. He was also President of the North West Aid Society at the time of his death.

Maude Levy married Percy Levy in 1920 and immediately started working for the Home. She was a founder member of the Ladies' Committee, and served on the House Committee until 1976. She gave many years of devoted care to the individual requirements of the residents. She was appointed Vice President in 1973. She died in 1991.

Their son, George Joseph Levy (1927–1966), was Chairman of the North West London Aid Society in 1955.

George Levy's son, Lewis Donald Levy (1910–1984), became Chairman of the North West Aid Society after the War, and later served the Society as President until 1984. He was Chairman of the Friends of Birchlands Hospital before the building became part of Nightingale.

Cecil Levy, a brother of Percy Levy, visited the Home regularly to help with the garden. He died in 1967.

Catherine, (Katie), a sister of Percy Levy, married Emil Stern. Their son David and his wife Joy first became members of the North West London Aid Society when, in 1938, they joined a Junior Section then known as the 'Young Hopefuls'. David was Chairman of the Aid Society in 1950 and has been its President since 1984.

He has been a Committee member of the Home for fifty years, and served as Deputy Chairman for forty-five years from 1953 to 1998. He was Chairman of the House Committee for nineteen years.

Since its inception in 1963, he has been identified with the North West London Aid Society's 'Housekeeper's Appeal' which is now sent out at Pesach. It takes the form of a small booklet. Each year a different item is attached to the front cover linked to an appropriate catch-phrase which enlists the donor's support in providing food for the residents.

Recently a penny was fixed to the front, with the words 'A penny for your kind thoughts'. Another time, a railway ticket for travel

'From Misery to Contentment via Nightingale' was sent out with the slogan 'Just the ticket – will you pay the fare?' The booklet contains tear-out pages for donating, for example, 100 lbs of potatoes for £20 or 250 lbs Matzos for £300.

With a number of others, mostly connected with Nightingale, David was a founder of Sunridge Court, a Jewish old people's residential home opened in 1970 in Golders Green, from which he recently retired as Chairman. He was succeeded by a member of the next generation of the family, Brian Levy, a son of Lewis Donald Levy, a former Chairman and current Vice President of the North West London Aid Society. Brian also served on the Applications Committee of Nightingale, and his sons and others of the sixth generation worked at the Annual Nightingale Bazaars.

David's brother Maxwell was treasurer of the Home's Annual Bazaar.

Maxwell's wife Anne Stern served on a number of committees from 1963 onwards, becoming Chairman of the Ladies' Committee in 1972 and Chairman of Nightingale House from 1977–1985.

Other relations were also involved. Lewis Levy's brother-in law, Moss Harris, a well-known antique dealer, was one of the founders of the Jewish Home of Rest and was Treasurer of Nightingale between the Wars.

Descendants of George Cohen are today involved with the charity – Sheila Brodtman is a member of the Executive Committee. She and her daughter serve on the Home Committee. Sheila and her husband have both served as Chairman of the North West London Aid Society.

From an historical perspective this pattern of charitable work is a perfect paradigm of how Jewish families and their relations worked in the community.

XVII

POST-WAR MODERNISATION

In 1945, Michael Slater was appointed Secretary (later Director) of the Home. Traditional and orthodox in religious matters, he proved to be a progressive and innovative administrator who helped forward the process of modernisation. He was assisted in his efforts by the medical officers and staff, who had often been important agents of change in the past, and by the committee members who were always keen to adopt the latest and best new ideas. There was also an increasing acceptance by the committee of the need for the Home to be more closely directed by professionals in the field of old age care. Slater, the staff, and committee, combined to remove all traces of institutionalism from the Home and make it a truly Jewish Home. They particularly concentrated their efforts upon improving facilities for the growing number of infirm residents.

The Annual Report of 1950 gave details of the progress that had been made since the end of the War:

> In a review of the reports for the past few years, one cannot fail to observe the trend towards the modern attitude to the care of the aged and infirm ... and to provide all the essentials of normal home life as far as the limitations of the present building allow. Recent visitors have been highly impressed by the freedom of movement accorded to the old people and by the brightness and homeliness of their surroundings. The provision of a room specially equipped for dental and chiropody treatment on the premises has proved a great boon to the residents. The question of providing physiotherapy treatment on the premises is receiving consideration. The introduction of occupational therapy is producing very good results, and has effected a notable change. Instead of a number of men and women sitting aimlessly about, there is now a cheerful band of workers happily engaged in many pleasurable activities ... The various articles they have made are displayed in a showcase placed in the hall of the Home and afford striking evidence of the skill and adaptability of some of the old folk who are very proud of their achievements. The beneficial effects of these occupational interests on

the general health of the residents cannot be over-estimated and are stressed in the Medical Officer's report.

It is believed that Nightingale was the first home of its kind to introduce occupational therapy on this scale.

It is not an exaggeration to say that the introduction of occupational therapy and physiotherapy revolutionised the lives of the residents. When the occupational therapy department was established in 1949, in makeshift accommodation, the therapist was not formally qualified. The department began to attract residents in greater numbers when a pre-fabricated annexe was opened, in 1952 and a full-time and qualified occupational therapist was appointed. Soon there was an average of sixty residents participating in the activities, and there was a waiting list.

Residents made rugs, lampshades, handbags, wallets, stools, scarves, soft toys, lace dinner sets, bath mats, tray cloths and baskets. Before long they were winning prizes for their work, including four prizes in the Handicraft Exhibition at Wandsworth Town Hall in 1957.

An early photograph of the department shows that the layout of the seating was not conducive to socialising, but this was soon remedied. By 1956, the importance of the social side of the occupational therapy was acknowledged and a bid was made to get even more residents involved. The number wanting to attend became greater than the accommodation allowed, so it was decided to form a Friendship Club that was founded by Miss Rose Rains who was involved until her death. It has proved to be a most important asset over the years. The Club facilitated the social reintegration of psychiatric patients who had been admitted into the Home that year.

In 1958 a 'weekly group musical circle' was instituted. This was held in the occupational therapy centre but also in the infirm wards. The need to get activities into the wards for those who were confined to them was becoming increasingly important.

The physiotherapy department was even more rudimentary. When it started it was not fully equipped, and its sole employee was a part-time physiotherapist. Nonetheless the department completed

763 treatments in 1952, rising to 4,000 the following year. Throughout the 1950s it extended its work and improved its range of treatments and equipment to hospital standards. Treatments in the mid-1950s sounded quite fearsome and included faradism, infra-red, wax-baths and various forms of remedial exercises.

A separate chiropody department had been introduced at the end of the war and by 1952 was treating about twelve patients weekly. One of the most important factors in the treatment of the aged is keeping them ambulant. Regular chiropodial treatments are important, particularly for those suffering from diabetes and arteriosclerosis. Having an in-house department was a boon.

The dentist reported that most of his time was spent on fitting dentures and promoting dental hygiene. Some residents resisted the idea of having dentures, but the dentist won many converts when, after he had made a number of successful fittings, others realised that the new teeth not only promoted better chewing but also improved their appearance, and made them look and feel younger.

By 1953, there were 146 residents at the Home. It soon became apparent to the Committee that if the Home were not expanded rapidly they would not be able to meet the demand. It was already well-established that the increase in demand for places in residential accommodation was due to increased longevity, itself partly due to the recent medical advances, and that longevity inevitably brought with it certain infirmities. The Home had prepared plans for a new wing that would include several beds for the infirm. Unfortunately the work, which it was hoped would start in 1950, was repeatedly postponed because of post-war shortages and restrictions. The shortages had been made worse as a result of the 1944 flying bomb attack on the Home of Rest. The part that included a ward reserved for Nightingale residents had been destroyed.

Until the building plans could be realised the management had to rely on making internal re-arrangements, and by doing so managed to increase the capacity from 146 to 155.

In 1954, a single-storey building was erected in the grounds to house nurses, and this released space in the main building and enabled the Home to increase the total to 169. Each new bed that could be added was vital. The Committee frequently had cause to lament the sheer desperation of many of their applicants – times were very hard for many lonely and frightened old people.

In 1953, the old wards were subdivided to give the residents a little more privacy, creating cubicles within the wards of just one, two or three beds. This, however, was only a partial solution as the ward dividers were seven feet in height and blocked sight but not noise.

The well-being of the residents was improved with the appointment, in 1956, of Mrs Muil as part-time Welfare Officer. Her task was to help solve the day-to-day problems, and relieve the anxieties of residents and new applicants. She became an extremely popular member of the staff, and this post has continued to be of great value to the Home.

By the mid-1950s it was apparent that the philosophy of care of the aged was changing rapidly. The Medical Officers embraced and promoted these changes whole-heartedly, and these must have been exciting times for the practitioners. The Medical Officer, Dr. Bernard Brest, said that greater priority would have to be given to the needs of infirm patients, to rehabilitate them to normal function, or as close to normal function as possible. He, and others like him, were turning their backs on the old regime under which the elderly were kept safely (and cheaply) in bed where they could rapidly deteriorate. Residents were now encouraged to leave the comfort of their beds during the day and become involved in the wide-ranging activities on offer. Even those who could no longer walk and had 'been tied to chairs for years', were suddenly finding themselves being taught to walk again. Retirement was taking on a different meaning.

Residents were allowed to have as many of their personal possessions with them as was practicable. The medical staff advocated and encouraged the introduction of homely elements. They also felt that maintaining a strong religious ethos and routine was very helpful for residents from a religious background.

In 1956, the Home experimented with receiving patients from mental hospitals who were deemed to have recovered from their illnesses. This did not amount to an annulment of the Home's normal policy of excluding patients suffering from a psychiatric illness. However, the Home had discovered that a number of aged Jews who had been kept for years in such hospitals made remarkable recoveries when they were taken into the Home, fed properly, and given activities in the occupational therapy department. For many their 'illness' had been caused solely by loneliness and lack of Jewish company.

The Home continued to run at a deficit, due to inexorably rising prices and wages. Expenditure in 1954 was nearly £42,000, the highest ever recorded to that date in the history of the Home, and it became necessary to eat into capital reserves that had been set aside for building purposes.

While the financial picture was somewhat gloomy, the Aid Societies continued to make then, as they do to this day, an important contribution to finances. The successful Brighton and Hove Society suspended its activities for the Home when the Brighton and Hove Home for the Aged opened, but this loss was compensated by the creation of three new Aid Societies in 1953, the Tudor, Chelsea, and Southend Aid Societies. The South-West London Society was resurrected in 1954, and for many years past has been organising annual garden fêtes and dinners and balls, raising large sums. The existing Aid Societies also remitted larger sums.

In November 1954 the Home ran a Bazaar at the Grosvenor House that raised a total of over £4,000. This event, organized by Mrs Edith (later Lady) Wolfson and her Joint Chairman Mrs Ruben Gold, under the Presidency of Mrs Ida Hyman, became a regular and most successful part of the fundraising calendar. Mrs Lily Rubin was Bazaar Chairman from 1971–98 and was very much in control of its organisation even when in her late eighties. Ruth Lady Wolfson took a great interest in the Bazaar, becoming its President, and is a generous supporter of Nightingale. Lily was latterly ably assisted by Priscilla Graham who became co-Chairman.

In 1954, the Home was finally able to make a start on its extension plans. The following Annual General Meeting was addressed by the Rev Dr A. Cohen, and an extract from his speech was reproduced in the Annual Report:

> Throughout the ages one prime cause of Jewish charity has been to help those aged who can no longer work for themselves and maintain

themselves because their strength has gone. It would be a sad day for any Jewish community which abandoned that traditional servitude ...

I forsee that in the coming years the demand for admission is going up by leaps and bounds and you will find that your resources are inadequate to meet the demand. This, therefore, is a problem which I commend to the earnest attention of the Jews in this city. First of all let them understand that they have this wonderful Home which for decades has been doing this remarkable work of providing a home for those who would be homeless. Let them see that the men and women who are devoting their energies and time to the carrying on of this Home are not hampered by deficits or have to go into a cheeseparing policy because they have to worry where the money is coming from to provide essentials.

I think I can say with confidence, whatever money the community will provide, whatever other homes we build, you by your tradition and experience have set a pattern which others can well follow.

Mr. Alfred Cope was appointed Chairman of the Rebuilding Fund Committee.

It was estimated that £200,000 would be required for the project. On 30 September 1956 Mr Cope laid the foundation stone in the presence of the Chief Rabbi, Israel Brodie, Patricia Hornsby-Smith MP, then the Parliamentary Secretary to the Ministry of Health, and a large gathering of distinguished guests.

The new wing, named the Jessie and Alfred Cope Wing, was completed in late 1957 and was ready for use in 1958. The Home could now accommodate 224 residents. 134 beds were set aside for infirm and semi-infirm residents of all types – senile, incontinent, and physically handicapped.

The building of the new wing was carried out concurrently with modernisation of the old building. Extra cubicles were constructed and other improvements made. Permanent lift attendants were employed to facilitate the movement of the residents.

One of the outstanding contributors to the progress of Nightingale in post war years has been Joseph N. (Joe) Cohen. Joe joined the Committee in 1950, and attended his last meeting fifty years later at the age of ninety-six, twelve years older that the average Nightingale resident.

The Synagogue.

(1)

(II)   *Visit of Prince Charles, 1976.*

Visit of Sarah, Duchess of York, 1991.

(III)

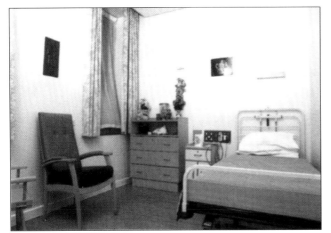

(V) *A typical bedroom.*

(VI) *Sabbath dinner.*

(VII) *One of the twelve dining rooms.*

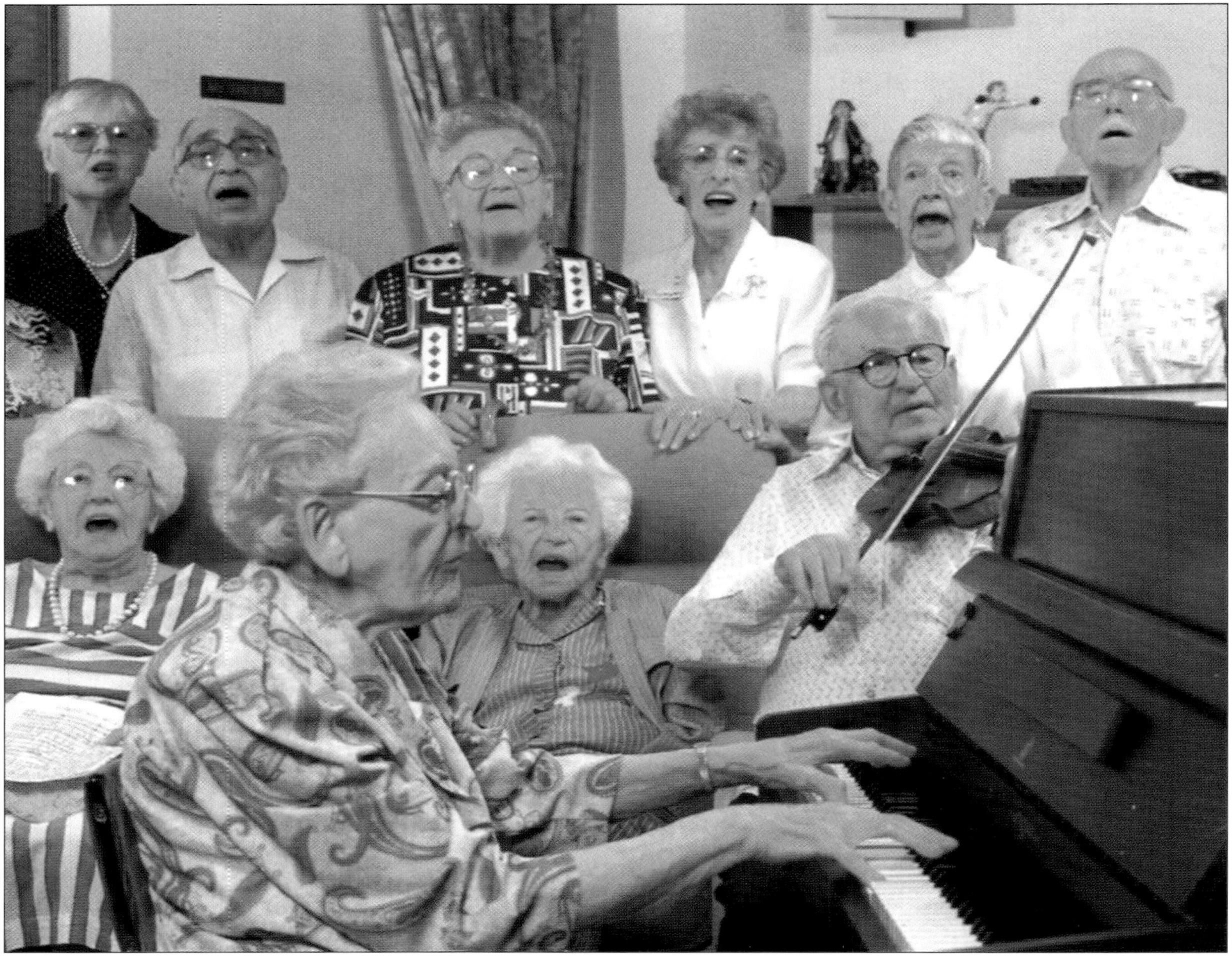

(VIII)
The Nightingale orchestra and chorus.

For this party in 2000, the staff wore their national costumes.

(IX)

He is a kindly and generous man, who has earned the affection and admiration of all his associates. Now a Vice President, his mind is as active as ever, but he did have to give up his golf a couple of years ago.

He was a Treasurer from 1963 to 1992, and following retirement regularly attended the meetings of the Treasurers and Trustees Committee where his sound advice was highly valued by his colleagues. He was a member of the House and Home Committees for twenty years. As Treasurer, he scrutinised carefully every significant item of expenditure, though he would readily support improvements and innovations for the benefit of the residents.

Joe was one of the founders of the Sunridge Court Residential Home and acted as Chairman for nearly thirty years. It was he who spotted the empty site in Golders Green on which Sunridge was built.

His late wife Ena started visiting Nightingale when she was seventeen and was a valued member of a number of committees over a period of more than fifty years until she retired in 1995 at the age of ninety-one. The Ena Cohen Conservatory has been named in her memory. It is attached to the David Clore Arts and Crafts Centre and, when not being used by the Gardening Club, forms a pleasant environment for relaxation.

Regular recreational activities continued. A highlight of 1953 was an outing to Westcliff-on-Sea for seventy residents as guests of Dalston and Stamford Hill Aid Society. They enjoyed a chicken lunch and high tea and were 'entertained by songs by Mrs. Epstein who was accompanied by a blind pianist'. In the same year a large party went to a variety show at the Palladium. The Coronation of 1953 was watched on the television at the Home and some of the residents were taken by bus to see the decorations.

A trolley-shop proved popular, and injected a feeling of normality, helping residents to establish stable patterns of behaviour, particularly where these had been disturbed by their move into the Home. The shop in its modern incarnation remains a very important facility in the Home.

1959 saw another innovation – visiting hours were extended. Residents could be visited outside of normal hours by arrangement, though this new dispensation still barred all visiting on the Sabbath and during festivals.

The 1950s were a revolutionary period in Nightingale's development. The whole regime of care was changed – and for the better. The foundations laid in that decade are still being built on and improved today. What was to follow was a great cycle of more than thirty years of physical rebuilding. This was undertaken to enable it to cater for the ever increasing demand for its care and loving attention. Unfortunately, Michael Slater did not survive to take his full part in this next phase of development.

XVIII

THE GREAT REBUILDING 1967–2000

In anticipation of Michael Slater's retirement, the Executive decided to appoint a Deputy Director who could work alongside him before taking over at an appropriate moment. Unfortunately, Michael died suddenly of a heart attack in 1963. In an appreciation of him given in the Synagogue on 11 March 1964, the Chairman, Cecil Kahn said that Michael was a truly religious man, not so much because he was very knowledgeable and regularly carried out the tenets of an orthodox Jew, but because he carried true religion into his everyday life. He was open-minded, and had a wonderful understanding and love of people as individuals. This endeared him to all who came into contact with him, whether belonging to the generation that had for the most part been brought up in Eastern Europe, or belonging to the later generation who had been educated in England. Asher Corren, a twenty-nine year old Israeli, was selected for the post.

At that time, the relationship between the Executive and the Director was very firmly that of employer and employee. It was expected that the Director and his staff would follow the Executive's instructions. They did not always see eye to eye. Cecil Kahn commented on this relationship:

> Committees are proverbially, and in fact, difficult to work under. Even so, if Michael did not agree with their decisions, or thought that someone was not being fairly treated, he would fight and fight hard for what he thought was right and fair. However, once a decision was taken, he would loyally abide by it, even if he disagreed. I am not going to say that he never tried to get such decisions changed at a later date if he thought it would be of benefit to the Home.

The Trustees together with Asher Corren disagreed profoundly with compulsory religious attendance and the restrictions on visiting hours on Sabbaths and festivals. The decision was taken to end them. The announcement of the immediate abolition of the compulsory wearing of kippot (regulation skull caps) and of attendance at religious services, caused a stir in the more orthodox quarters of the Home. Televisions were allowed to be used in residents' private rooms on Sabbath and the festivals, as many became fretful and upset at being denied it. The sets remained switched off in the public rooms. Visiting rules were relaxed, visits on Saturdays and Festivals now being permitted.

The Medical Staff consisted of a Matron, her deputy, twelve qualified staff, and thirty State Enrolled Nurses and Orderlies. Matron, an all important figure, was then in charge of administering the domestic and kitchen staff in addition to her normal duties. She was relieved of this onerous extra responsibility in 1969 when a house-keeper caterer was recruited.

Throughout the decade there was a heavy demand for the services of the Home. The average age of applicants was eighty, and the incidence of infirmity continued to rise. In 1967 half the residents were classified as infirm; in 1968 sixty per cent were, and whereas ten years earlier it was rare to find a resident over ninety years of age, in 1968 thirty-five of the 279 residents had passed ninety.

The largest category of residents consisted of those who could not look after themselves. There were also those who were lonely, and those who, for one reason or another, could no longer be cared for by their families. Nightingale fully understood the stresses and strains of caring for an aging parent, (most particularly on a daughter or daughter-in-law), perhaps in a small flat or house. It appreciated that various conflicts of interest could arise in such situations – such as a grandchild wanting to play records, it being a well-known fact that the young have poor hearing and must therefore have the record player turned on to full volume – while a grandparent sought some peace and quiet.

The application process for prospective residents ran on broadly similar lines to earlier years. Some of the cases that had come before the Investigating Committee were described by Cecil Kahn in his 1967 Report:

> A dear old couple crippled with old age trying to look after each other in an upstairs room with water and toilet several floors below.

Not a relative in the world, and too shaky in the legs to go out to buy her own food.

A very old man having to share his teenage grandson's bedroom in a two-roomed flat – not very hygienic, nor fair to the boy working for a scholarship.

Living with married daughter who ought to be in hospital for a serious operation but cannot leave her mother.

Nowhere else to go except to stay in the mental hospital although, after treatment, now quite normal.

The wife's father, the husband's mother, and two children, all six in a small tenement flat – hardly conducive to a happy marriage or to mentally stable children.

As Cecil Kahn commented, it seemed hardly creditable that in the days of the welfare state such cases were typical of those reported to the monthly investigation meeting when the Committee had to select, from a large list, those most needy for admission to the few empty beds available.

When a new Constitution was adopted by Nightingale in 1952, Cecil became the Home's first Chairman, a position which he held for twenty-six years. Under his Chairmanship, and largely through his initiative, Nightingale carried out the most extensive scheme of modernisation and expansion in its entire history. This started with the addition of the Cope Wing, included the Rayne House flatlets, and ended with the opening of the magnificent Red Brick Extension. In all, during his term of office, the number of residents grew from 146 to 381.

In 1969, the weekly cost of maintaining each resident was £13.13.1d., and the annual cost of running the Home £153,000. Local authority funding, plus the resident's state pension, covered 58% of the cost. Though the Home had to find the excess, this subsidy was undoubtedly a significant factor in promoting the Home's stability and growth.

Advances in care were maintained and greatly extended. The medical rooms and departments were improved, and more staff were provided for care of the infirm. Some day rooms were provided in the wards.

In 1960, Dr Cyril Josephs was appointed as deputy to the

Medical Officer, Dr Bernard Brest, and he brought further energy and ideas, complementing those introduced by Brest. When Josephs took over as Medical Officer in 1965, a position he held for several decades, he demonstrated exceptional qualities of care and innovation. He held strong views on euthanasia, being vehemently against its use. Some argued that provided suitable safeguards were introduced, it should be permissible to end a life at the express wish of someone who had found living no longer tolerable. Josephs considered this view fraught with danger. He believed that a person who was suffering was rarely able to give a dispassionate opinion, and his or her wish could alter when circumstances changed. He was a firm believer that Nightingale should respect its Jewish ethos, that where there is life there is hope. He quoted a case in which an elderly lady, severely disabled with paralysis of one arm and leg, had calmly told him that life was no longer worth living and she wanted to die. She was at a clinic that he held on Fridays. 'I told her that I never killed people on Fridays, and that we could discuss the matter again after the occupational therapist and the team of physiotherapists had seen her'. They met some weeks later in the occupational therapy department where she was busily working at *petit point*, doing the most intricate and beautiful needlework with the one hand she could use. He asked her if she still wanted to die and she replied, 'certainly not before I have finished my needlework, and I am a slow worker'. Another lady in a similar situation said she had changed her mind and wanted to carry on at least until she had finished reading her library books.

Formal and informal exchanges of information were encouraged with local hospitals, the local authorities, the Jewish Welfare Board and other care organisations, and with the many visitors from around the world who came to see the Home. The policy of keeping residents active and out of bed, and helping themselves as much as possible, was pursued and accelerated with full vigour.

The great need to cater for yet more infirm elderly residents and, importantly, to separate the different types of resident, was by now clearly established. Radical changes were introduced. The most able were separately accommodated from the physically infirm; those with psychiatric problems formed their own group. The Home was divided into smaller units to create a more homely and welcoming environment. To emphasise just how much it was a real home and not an institution, it was decided to change the name from Home for Aged Jews to the more acceptable 'Nightingale House'. Today the Home is most commonly known simply as 'Nightingale'.

In 1965, the nurses' bungalow was converted and provided accommodation for eleven active residents in their own quarters. A major building project came to fruition in 1967 when Rayne House was built on a plot of land in Sudbrooke Road, purchased with money donated by Lord Rayne in honour of his parents Phillip and Deborah on the occasion of their Golden Wedding Anniversary. It consisted of a group of twenty-four self-contained flatlets for residents, including two for married couples, who wanted to look after themselves and were fit enough to do so. The flats were warden controlled, and residents could use all the facilities of Nightingale as, when, and if they wanted to. It was based on research that showed that this sort of independence helped the elderly healthy to be active and happy. By 1968, a complete reorganisation had been carried out. It was little realised at the time that the building of Rayne House marked just the beginning of a hectic thirty years of rebuilding work that would totally transform Nightingale's entire fabric.

Financially, Nightingale was operating at a stable level of deficit, despite rising costs. Fundraising continued successfully, and two new Aid Societies were created in the 1960s; the Clapton and the Stamford Hill Aid Societies.

As in the 1950s, residents were entertained with concerts, excursions and film shows. Strenuous efforts were made to involve them in outdoor activities such as croquet. Steps were taken to improve the quality of the meals which could be rather indifferent. A Menu Committee was formed, and a little more money was spent on the food. Generous donors were encouraged to form clubs such as the 52 Club and the Vienna Club, to provide the appreciative residents with expensive treats such as smoked salmon and a weekly delivery of viennas from Bloom's Restaurant.

In 1968, Alfred Cope retired as President, the post he had occupied since 1955. A man of immense capability, he greatly improved the standing of Nightingale and its facilities during his term of office. He had served the Home in various capacities for fifty years. If he saw that something needed doing to improve conditions he would sometimes offer to pay for it himself. It was because he was so generous that he was able to call on his friends to support him, and he attracted many new donors to the Home. J. B. Rubens, also a generous supporter, succeeded him and served between 1968–1970.

The numbers of infirm steadily grew. In 1971, two-thirds of all the residents required nursing care. They had an average stay of about three and a half years and passed away at an average age of eighty-six.

In the 1970s, hyper-inflation hit the country, and consequently Nightingale's finances. The introduction of Value Added Tax in 1972 was an added burden. The worst effects of inflation were felt between 1974 and 1976. Commodity prices soared, and wages were forecast to rise by up to eighty per cent in the following two years.

Local Authorities were still making per capita grants for residents, and these now covered up to 75% of costs, but the authorities started to feel the squeeze of inflation and became more cautious about accepting this optional liability.

Notwithstanding the financial difficulties, the Home still managed to increase the accommodation necessary to meet the ever expanding demand for places, some of which was caused by inflation eating into pensioners' savings. Most importantly, the Committee set itself the strategic aim of providing fully integrated care so that residents, once admitted, would never have to leave the Home, whatever the state of their health.

This called for a massive building programme. In 1973 a two acre plot adjacent to the Home was purchased from the Inner London Educational Authority at a cost of £67,000. It was part of the land that had been occupied since 1899 by the Jews' Deaf and Dumb Home, later called The Residential School for Jewish Deaf Children. Completed in 1976, the building erected on the site was originally called the 'Red Brick Extension', renamed the 'Gerald Lipton Centre' in May 2001. Major benefactors of the project included Sir Michael Sobell, Sir Charles Clore and Barnett Shine.

This was an advanced facility for its time, carried out after extensive research in Scandinavia and the United States, and after advice had been sought from the Centre for Policy for the Aging. It was designed by an enterprising and innovative architect, Barry Edwards of the George Watt Partnership.

What distinguished it was its size – at a stroke it almost doubled the available accommodation. The design was revolutionary in that it consisted of 160 single rooms, each with a private toilet and shower, on four residential floors, each floor having its own dining room. Cecil Kahn, Asher Corren and the Committee felt that residents could be better cared for in the dignity and privacy of private rooms.

There were three wings, like the spokes of a wheel. In principle, on each floor there were to be three groups of between twelve and fifteen residents, each with its own utility area where the group could make cups of tea and sit and chat. The layout created a 'village' atmosphere. The ground floor had various recreation rooms, including separate television rooms for each channel. The idea was that residents would be able to form friendships, firstly with their near neighbours in the same wing, secondly with the remaining occupants of their floor, and finally with the even wider group to be found on the ground floor. Furthermore the circulation up and down the building would be beneficial.

By this division into several smaller self-contained units, all functioning under one organisation, Nightingale was coming into line with the general trend for smaller homes. Despite this, many in the Jewish community, and in the care profession, criticized its size. It was said that Nightingale had become too large, and some maintained that single rooms were an unnecessary expense that would prove uneconomical. Time has shown that the concept was exactly right for the Home. Economies of scale were achieved, and the basis was created for further expansion of facilities for the residents.

Nightingale was honoured when Prince Charles agreed to open the building. It was his first public engagement after he left the Navy. His driver lost his way and gave the Prince a fascinating but unrepeatable tour of Balham. Despite this, the Prince managed to arrive and complete his duties. Wearing a decorative kippah, a gift from the Home's President Cecil Elsom, the Prince showed great interest in the Home and all that he saw. The *Daily Mail* ran the headline, 'Where Did You Get That Hat?' The Prince had jokingly remarked that if he were to put his naval cap down on the ground it would probably attract a greater contribution than this gift.

The visit was a great psychological boost for the Home and all connected with it – they really felt as if they had arrived at last. The memory of this royal visit, and others since, have undoubtedly had a permanent and very positive effect on the Home.

Nightingale was very fortunate in this period to have the support from within the community of the services of a number of distinguished benefactors who were also key players, including Sir Charles Abrahams KCVO, President of the charity from 1970–1972, and subsequently a Vice President. He and his wife Luisa were good and generous friends to the Home. He introduced HRH the Prince of Wales and HRH the Duke of Edinburgh to Nightingale. He was a supporter of the Duke of Edinburgh's Award Scheme, and Prince Philip was represented at his memorial service held in the Home.

Morris Leigh Ph.D., a Vice President of the Home and a generous supporter made a major contribution to many building and development projects, working closely with Cecil Elsom. He and his wife provided the excellent Manja and Morris Leigh Succah, a permanent building which doubles as a billiards room throughout the rest of the year. It replaced the former temporary Succah that needed to be erected, dismantled, and stored every year.

Jack Sampson too took an active part in the management of the Home, and served on the Executive Committee.

Cecil Elsom CBE FRIBA has a special place in the history of Nightingale, serving as President from 1974 to 1996. The distinguished architect became involved through Lord Rayne, who was the first patron of the Home. From the 1970s to the present day, Cecil has been an advisor and driving force behind much of the development and redevelopment work.

One of the brightest stars during this period was David Clore, a brother of Sir Charles Clore. David was a distinguished member of the community and became the chief fundraiser for the extension, and beyond. His philosophy was that one could as a benefactor support many charities, but could devote oneself only to one.

Fortunately for Nightingale, he chose it as his main cause and throughout the 1970s and early 1980s proved to be extraordinarily successful. 'He badgered. He cajoled. He never missed a trick and yet, when he had extracted a large donation from a member of the Community, they still had to smile and admit that they loved him.' David Clore's son Charles is today the enthusiastic Chairman of the North West London Aid Society.

When completed, the Red Brick Extension made the other facilities look dated and inferior in comparison. What had started as a minor scheme to redecorate the Main building, led to a complete modernisation. One is reminded of the story of the man who set out to replace one piece of damaged wallpaper and ended up rebuilding his house. A plan was drawn up to renew the old building and devote it to the care of those with psychiatric problems; the remaining major facilities were to be replaced and upgraded. During the 'redecoration' an entire temporary building, the brainchild of Asher Corren, was built to accommodate residents who moved out while work was done, thus allowing business to carry on as usual. This was no mean feat, and Cecil Elsom said he had never before seen this scale of work carried out while all the facilities remained open.

Work started on the Davis, Franklin, and Alfred Cope Wings in 1977 and ended in 1980 with the refurbishment of the whole of the ground floor, including the Synagogue. There was a new shop, hairdressing salon, physiotherapy department, dental centre, the Miriam and David Clore Medical Centre, a new entrance hall, and the Lady (Edith) Wolfson Rehabilitation Centre for which the Wolfson Foundation donated significant amounts.

In 1979, the Home suffered the loss of Mrs Ida Hyman, the daughter of Moss Harris. She had been associated with the Home for over sixty years, and was a co-founder of the Jewish Home of Rest. At Nightingale she served as Chairman of the Ladies' Committee, was a member of the Executive Committee, and latterly a Vice-President of the Home.

The struggle to establish the Jewish Home of Rest had begun in 1904, led by Reverend A. A. Green. There was no Jewish institution at that time that would accept those who had no hope of recovering from their illness, tuberculosis being the principal cause for

concern. Reverend Green said that 'the lot of the dying consump-
tive poor is terribly sad. The great hospitals, anxious to reserve
their beds for curable cases, will not retain them. There is nothing
before them but the cruel alternative of either dying at home, and
infecting all their surroundings, or ending their days in the
workhouse infirmary'. After years of unsuccessful attempts to raise
funds, the breakthrough came in 1925 when Ernest Franklin, the
President, and other officers of the Home for Aged Jews, offered
Rev Green and his supporters a piece of land at the rear of their
own buildings, an offer gratefully accepted. The Home of Rest
opened in July 1927 and catered for two classes of patients – those
suffering from a disease that had ceased to respond to hospital
treatment and who, because they suffered from a terminal illness
were not qualified for admission to the Jewish Home for Incurables;
and those disqualified on medical grounds from admission to the
Home for Aged Jews. Bernhard Baron was a major contributor to
both the Home of Rest and Nightingale.

Birchlands had been nationalised in 1948 when the National
Health Service Act came into force, and was removed from the
ownership of the Jewish community. From then until 1979 it was
run as a hospital for terminally ill, mainly Jewish, patients.
Nightingale was allowed to purchase it, using money provided by
Lord Rayne in memory of his father Phillip Rayne. To some extent,
this could be considered as a return to its rightful owners. During
the subsequent rebuilding the Harry and Abe Sherman Foundation
were among the most generous supporters. It was gutted and
remodelled to provide single and double rooms, an additional fifty-
nine beds for the infirm.

In November 1980, the building was opened by a second royal
visitor, the Duke of Edinburgh. He said he was extremely
impressed with the facilities and the obvious happiness of the
residents. He unveiled a commemorative plaque after the Chief
Rabbi, Immanuel (later Lord) Jakobovits had explained to him the
history of the mezuzah (a parchment inscribed with religious texts
and attached in a case to the doorpost of a Jewish house).

During the 1980s, Nightingale, against the prevailing mainstream view, continued steadfastly with its principles of 'service',
and 'mutual social responsibility in action' towards the older
members of the community, by intensifying its efforts to increase

the number of single rooms. The watchwords of the Home were 'dignity, comfort, happiness'. The Home affirmed that its duty was to care for the whole person not just his physical needs.

Nightingale continued to serve a progressively older clientele; in 1987 the average age of the residents was a remarkable eighty-eight years. The 1980s did nothing to shorten the lengthy waiting lists or the demand for infirm beds and more specialised medical care. Residents continued to be streamed by medical status. Most importantly, with rare exceptions, medical facilities were available to ensure that each and every resident could look forward to a lifelong stay.

Following heightened tension in the Middle East in 1982, Nightingale employed full-time security staff. A high level of security continues to the present day with security guards on duty and CCTV protection.

A highlight of 1983 was the visit of a youthful Princess Diana. She had originally planned a fairly short visit, but stayed on for a considerable time as she wanted to see more and more. All were most struck by her interest, her natural approach to the residents, her sympathy, and genuine compassion. Princess Diana was living in Buckingham Palace at the time and was asked by one of the residents, 'Where do you live?' 'Not far from here', she replied. The verdict of the players in a card school with whom she chatted was that the Princess was 'an Ace'.

To safeguard itself against the risk that the government might reduce or completely suspend its funding, and to protect the future maintenance and fabric of the Home, a special endowment fund, known as The Friends of Nightingale, was set up by David Clore in 1983, an example of his farsightedness. The worst financial fears were not realised, but applicants for admission to the Home no longer automatically received maintenance from their Local Authority, many of which had to cut back on expenditure. As a result, the Home frequently had to work hard and long to secure individual funding. There were also cutbacks in funding by the Department of Health and Social Security.

The Fund was launched with a special dinner at Blenheim Palace, the first kosher dinner there. In 1985, a major ball was held at the Hilton Hotel for 650 people. The Guildhall dinner of 1987, at which Dr David Owen, the former Foreign Secretary (now Lord Owen) was the principal speaker, raised one million pounds.

1985 brought sadness to the Home with the deaths during the year of David Clore, Anne Stern, and Sir Charles Abrahams, all of whom had been steadfast supporters. David Clore had devoted himself to charitable causes from an early age. During World War I he collected odd cigarettes to give to soldiers. Not just a fundraiser and a man of vision, he was involved in the day to day running of the Home, aiding both staff and management. He also concerned himself with the residents, taking time to get to know them better. At his passing a resident wrote:

> But though we feel his presence
> There is an empty place
> At the table –
> For David

His widow, Irene, carried on his tradition of support for the Home.

Following the untimely deaths in 1985 of Anne Stern and David Clore, Gerald Lipton was persuaded by colleagues to allow his name to go forward as the new Chairman. He was duly appointed to this position, a post that he held until his retirement on 1 January 2001. In his youth he had been introduced by Alfred Cope to the Ezra Society, one of the most successful of the Aid Societies, and soon became involved in fundraising on Nightingale's behalf. By 1985, he was already a long time supporter. In the early 1980s he had accepted David Clore's invitation to become more involved, and joined the Executive and Finance Committees.

That year, Nightingale changed its form of registration under the new legislation to a dual registration, as both a 'Nursing Home' and a 'Residential Home', reflecting the ever increasing level of nursing care that was undertaken. This led to even more inspections, and the implementation of additional regulatory improvements in safety, hygiene and fire precautions.

Also that year, the valuable role played by Leon Smith over the years as Asher Corren's right-hand man was recognised. His official title was changed from Assistant Director to Deputy Director. Corren wrote, 'In many ways it is a formal recognition of the work that he has been doing. He has earned the respect and the affection of everyone at the Home. He plays a strategic role in every aspect of our work'.

The Home continued to liaise with a variety of organisations and individuals. It was affiliated to the Central Council for Jewish Social Services, and had contacts with the Centre for the Policy on Aging and with the British Council who arranged visits of medical staff from Norway and Sweden. There were visits by Directors of overseas homes, by social workers, and by many others. The continuing exchange of ideas and expertise is always invaluable. On a local level Nightingale is registered with Wandsworth Health Authority and the London Borough of Wandsworth and enjoys a constructive and harmonious relationship with both.

In 1986, the David Clore Arts and Crafts Centre was opened, replacing the existing pre-fab that was now too small. It is a permanent, architect-designed building with a roof supported by striking laminated wood beams, and provides the most up-to-date facility of its kind. Many consider it the crown jewel of the Home. It is used by up to 100 residents each day, many participating in the group activities on offer. Expert instruction is available, and there is an array of up-to-date computers that are well used by the 'silver-surfers'.

The Centre was funded in David Clore's memory by the Clore Foundation. A dinner in David's honour brought an overwhelming response from those who not only came to honour David, but who also gave money for the David Clore Memorial Fund which was set up to help balance the books.

The Clore family have proved themselves to be outstandingly generous supporters of Nightingale, and continue to be so. A bust of Sir Charles sits proudly in the boardroom to commemorate his munificence. This generosity has been carried on by his daughter, Dame Vivien Duffield, an incomparable supporter and wonderful friend of the Home who has made many appeals at major fundraising dinners. To the delight of her many friends at Nightingale she consented to be a patron, a position she now occupies with distinction.

It is appropriate to mention here Mrs Mary Nathan, one of those to whom this book is dedicated. She was first introduced to Nightingale in the early 1970s, and initially became involved with the shop, which at that time was being run by Anne Stern, Chairman of the Ladies' Committee. In due course Mary became a member of that Committee and subsequently a member of the House Committee. She took over the chairmanship of the Home Committee, a position she held to the late 1990s. Her special interest is the medical welfare of the residents, and she is a key member of the clinical services working group. She is well known and greatly respected by residents, (all of whom she knows personally), relatives and staff alike.

Mary is a discreet and sensitive hands-on volunteer who has assisted and supported the Home in many ways. For the past three years she has been the Deputy Chairman of Nightingale. Mary has devoted an enormous amount of time to the Home and its residents over many, many years and has been of huge support to both the past and current management and is an integral and vital member of the Executive and Finance Committee.

XIX

THE CLOSING YEARS OF THE
TWENTIETH CENTURY

During the past twenty years Nightingale has continued to enrich its residents with every manner of mental and physical stimulation. The Social Activities organisers arrange a phenomenal range of events, including Yiddish and Hebrew Classes, a cultural class run by the London Jewish Cultural Centre, Shiurim (discussions) conducted by Rabbis, museum and gallery outings, trips to the opera, and theatre musical evenings. The Home is richly supported by a host of celebrity speakers and entertainers. The Duke of Edinburgh recently said 'sign me up' when he saw the programme available to residents.

Edwina Currie, a former government minister, has been very successful with a club called 'Hooked on Books'. A group of women, all in their nineties or late eighties meets every six weeks. They have strong likes and dislikes, and all are well read, in some cases in four, five or six languages. A recent visitor to the Club was Jenny Hartley, the daughter of former Chairman Anne Stern and author of the recently published *Who belongs to Reading Groups?*' She noted that physically frail though the Club members might be – 'they wheeled, zimmered, and hobbled in' – their minds were razor-sharp and the atmosphere was electric. One member told her, 'Just because maybe you can't see or hear too well, you still want to read and to talk'. On the day Jenny visited, the guest speaker was P. D. James. Everyone contributed to the discussion, and sometimes members had to be forcibly silenced. For these women reading is a pleasure they have enjoyed for eighty or ninety years, and continue to enjoy.

Religious activities continue to be strongly supported in the beautiful Synagogue, and residents participate in, and help to run them. The festivals are celebrated with gusto, and the Home is particularly impressive at Pesach when there are twelve simultaneous seders conducted with the assistance of volunteers. Very simple 'mini' seders are held for those with severe dementia, a particularly compassionate idea. While it may be difficult to know with certainty what impact such a seder has on a sufferer, it is believed that it does communicate something of value even to the most confused of residents. It is worth noting that though many of the Honorary Officers and senior management have been members of Reform and Liberal synagogues, this has never affected the orthodox character of the Home.

Potential residents by now expected higher standards, and had different needs that could not be met in the original Edwardian extensions to *Ferndale*. The Davis and Franklin wings were outmoded, and the position of the staircases made it impossible for lifts to be installed. In 1987, the wings were replaced by the new Balint Wing, named after a family renowned for their generosity. The Andrew Balint Charitable Trust, the George Balint Charitable Trust, and the Paul Balint Charitable Trust, have been exceptionally kind to Nightingale over many years, and their support has been invaluable.

The new wing was designed to take infirm or mentally frail men and women in need of nursing care. It has single and double rooms for forty-four men and women. It was opened in 1990 by Chief Rabbi Lord Jakobovits who was accompanied by the Rt. Hon. Anthony Newton, OBE the Secretary of State for Social Security, and by members of the Balint family. This phase of building also introduced the new Max Astaire Coffee Lounge that provided the residents with a pleasant place to meet friends and to socialise.

January 1990 saw the death of Cecil Kahn, the Chairman of the Home from 1952 to 1978. A Cambridge graduate, successful businessman, very clever and far seeing, he was a 'hands-on' operator. During his term of office he was very much in charge of the Home with which he had been involved since 1924. He also served the Jewish Home of Rest where he was Chairman before it was taken over by the National Health Service in 1948. He later became a member of the Regional Hospital Board and of the House and Finance Committee of his local Cheshire Home. He was a founder member of the Committee of Sunridge Court. An out-standing supporter he was to be much missed by Nightingale.

The 1990's proved to be an especially challenging decade. Drastic changes in funding resulted from the implementation by the government in April 1993 of the Community Care Act. During the 1980's, it was becoming apparent to Government that the cost of providing care for older members of the community was soaring due to the ever increasing numbers of elderly people in the general population who needed to be in residential homes or offered more support at home. A growing band of private residential homes were established to meet this need. Many were excellent, but some were simply taking advantage of a money-making opportunity through the relatively easily available government subsidies.

The government decided to remove the burden from its own shoulders by devolving responsibility for the care of the elderly to the Local Authorities. Central Government would no longer provide direct funding, but instead distribute it via the local authorities. Problems then arose because the funds were not ring-fenced. For the first time, the cost of providing care for older members of the community came into direct competition with other areas within local authority budgets. Money saved by local authorities on the care of the elderly could be used by them to cover shortages elsewhere. Some local authorities with inadequate budgets considered care of the elderly to be of secondary importance, and were reluctant to fund residential care places, using the cheaper option of home support services instead. Many local authority homes were closed.

Sadly, when assessing the need for residential care, local councils did not take into account the serious loneliness suffered by many elderly applicants forced to remain at home through lack of mobility, most of whose friends had died or were no longer able to visit.

From its implementation in 1993, the Community Care Act created a burdensome degree of bureaucracy. The Home now had to deal with thirty-five separate purchasing boroughs, each of which had its own criteria for admission, each of which had its own separate tendering contracts and documentation, and each of which was offering different sums of money for care. In some ways it was reminiscent of the boundaries dispute that followed the poor laws of 1834, a dreadful commentary on its effect.

Unacceptable delays in assessment caused serious distress to applicants. The Home found itself tied up with much more administration, and as a result rooms were sometimes left vacant whilst the bureaucratic machine ground its way forward. It was no surprise that this change in the law immediately created financial difficulties for the Home. Reductions had to be made in staff through natural wastage, and more flexible and effective working practices were introduced. The changes to funding along with rising costs were part of the reason for a £1.8 million deficit in 1994.

It should be stressed that the implementation of the Community Care legislation of 1993 was probably one of the single biggest influences on life at Nightingale in generations. The direct effect was very quickly to alter the profile of incoming residents. People were now greatly encouraged and facilitated to stay in their own homes for very much longer. The knock-on effect of this was that by the time people did come into Nightingale, and left their own homes, they were very much older, and frailer, physically and mentally, and more highly dependent than would otherwise have been the case.

Nightingale has had to adjust itself to this new reality. Whereas previously Nightingale had taken escorted trips to Israel, it was no longer able to do so. The number of coach trips to the coast has been reduced because there are fewer active residents able to benefit from them. This, in turn, has necessitated an increase in nursing and paramedical staff to cope with increasing levels of dependency.

A highlight of 1991 was another royal visit, by the Duchess of York. She was well received by residents, Committee, and staff alike. The Duchess had come to see the Home in preparation for a dinner to be held that evening at the Guildhall. Although it had not been expected that she would speak at the dinner, she was so impressed by what she had seen that she insisted on doing so, and won the hearts of those present with her sincerity.

The Jessie and Alfred Cope Wing that had been built to the highest standards of its time had no separate facilities. By 1992 the wing was overcrowded and by contemporary standards had poor facilities. It was redesigned, modernised and extended to accommodate thirty-four residents who needed specialised nursing in single and double rooms. The redeveloped wing was reopened that year by Tim Yeo the then Parliamentary Under Secretary for Health, in the presence of Chief Rabbi, Professor Jonathan Sacks. The Chief Rabbi has been an extremely supportive friend of Nightingale. Always willing to help in any way possible, he and his wife Elaine have visited Nightingale on many occasions.

It should be emphasised that not a single penny was contributed by Government towards the capital cost of this, or indeed any other of the buildings that have been described in this book.

Other areas of the Home remained in need of updating or restoration. Some of the old Victorian wards were still in use in 1996 in the original main building – a usage regarded as a 'blemish' on the Home. To remove it was a prime aim of Gerald Lipton. It was clearly unacceptable, especially as it was now official Government policy that residents should be in single rooms. It had long been recognised that this stage of redevelopment would be most complex as it would involve shutting down and relocating the very heart of the Home.

A detailed logistical operation then swung into place; the Medical Centre, physiotherapy and occupational therapy departments, and the administrative offices, were all put into temporary accommodation in the garden. To offset the considerable loss of beds resulting from the conversion of the old wards into single rooms, the Gerald Lipton Centre was extended to provide twenty-eight single rooms in the new Asher Corren Wing.

Once the way was clear, the old building was gutted from top to bottom and rebuilt. The multi-bedded rooms and some wards that had held as many as seventeen people were eliminated. The new accommodation contained single rooms each with private facilities. Gerald Lipton had achieved his aim. The total cost was £4.5m. To complete the changes the beautiful gardens were relandscaped, thanks to the generosity of Mina and Everard Goodman, and Joy and Stanley Cohen OBE.

The most recent project has been the total upgrading of the Gerald Lipton Centre itself. In addition to straightforward renovation and redecoration, substantial adaptations had to be made to cater for residents who were older and frailer than those for whom the building had originally been designed. The Duke of Edinburgh honoured Nightingale with a second visit when, in May 2001, he renamed the Red Brick Building the Gerald Lipton Centre.

Also during the 1990s there were innovations in the psychological care for the residents. A part-time counsellor was appointed in 1991, and a year's music therapy for the residents was provided by The Doron Foundation. 'Reminiscence' sessions were introduced in 1994. Groups handle and discuss objects that they were familiar with in their youth, such as the old fashioned heavy flat iron. It is an intriguing development that has been extremely therapeutic for those taking part, pleasantly rekindling old memories and associations.

The task of raising money for essential improvements is, of course, a relentless never-ending challenge that constantly has to be faced by the Executive and Finance Committee. Nightingale has been fortunate that over many years it has been the recipient of major financial assistance from the Charles Wolfson Charitable Trust, the Archie Sherman Charitable Trust and, more recently, from the American based Harry and Jeanette Weinberg Foundation.

Nightingale's finances received a further boost in 1995 when Hyman Davidson, on his own behalf and on behalf of his late brother Alec, made a gift to Nightingale of a substantial building consisting of retail units with office space in the downtown colonial area of Charleston, South Carolina.

Throughout its long history Nightingale has received donations, large and small, from trusts, companies, and individuals. The contributions made by the Aid Societies, from the oldest, the North West London and the South West London, to the most recently formed, have been of inestimable value. This book has highlighted some of the major gifts and the efforts made to obtain them, but these should not be allowed to overshadow the many other gifts that have been received, each of which is equally appreciated. Nightingale needs them all if it is to achieve its aim of maintaining the high standard of care it provides for its residents.

On 31 December 1997 an era ended when Asher Corren retired from the post that he had held in such a distinguished manner for thirty-five years. In addition to his many other contributions to

Nightingale, he was responsible for much of the development at the Home, and was a great success as a fundraiser. Leon Smith his deputy of many years standing took over and is now making his mark on the life of the Home. Leon combines his great care for all the residents of the Home with a considerable administrative and strategic flair.

When he took over he found himself in a qualitatively different environment from Asher Corren. The Community Care Act had only recently made its full impact. For the first time in the history of the Home there was not a huge waiting list for places. The need was, and is, still there, but many find it impossible to obtain funds from the local authorities. The condition imposed of selling off one's home to qualify for help has been widely criticised and is a severe discouragement to many older people who are now resentful. Having paid a life-time of contributions to the government to provide for others, they feel the government has failed to provide for them in their own hour of need.

During the time of Gerald Lipton's Chairmanship it was not uncommon for him to be seen at Nightingale, meeting informally with groups of residents to ask what they thought of the food, or to ask their suggestions on ways in which various aspects of the running and care of the home could be improved. His experience was an enormous help in the management of the Home which by now was a medium sized business, with a turnover in excess of £10m, and a staff of some 350.

An organisation of this size requires capable treasurers to ensure that money is wisely and economically spent, and Nightingale has always been extremely well served in this department. Particular mention must be made of Mark Gordon, a chartered accountant by profession, who was Senior Treasurer from 1977–1993, and whose dedication to Nightingale was boundless.

Under Gerald's Chairmanship, others who have become active in the management of the Home include Brian Barnett, Leonard Green, Keith Goodman, and Senior Treasurer Maurice Lawson who masterminded the recent intricate refurbishment programme, and who continues in that role. He devotes a great deal of his time to Nightingale, concentrating on the development of the building as well as on his financial role. Whenever there is a new project, he is the first to put his name forward to assist. His family too, have been very generous supporters of the Home.

Gerald raised many millions of pounds for Nightingale over the period of his Chairmanship enabling the massive redevelopment throughout the complex to be made without affecting the Home's reserves. Gerald also helped to bring the work of Nightingale to the attention of the wider community.

During his term of office, Nightingale developed into a non-bureaucratic flexible organisation capable of responding quickly to people's needs. He is particularly proud that it is led by a powerful team of laymen and professionals, and that it has maintained its independence while fostering and maintaining even closer links with the major organisations in the field of care for the older person.

David Clore had created a close association between Nightingale and the Western Marble Arch Synagogue, and Gerald, who is an elder of the Synagogue, has strengthened the bond.

A unique contribution has been made to Nightingale by Gerald and he continues to do so today in his new role as President.

His successor as Chairman of the Home is the well-known community figure, Rosalind Preston O.B.E., who has undertaken the task of carrying on the great traditions of the Home.

XX

A PERSPECTIVE

Those who have been involved with the Home for many years would doubtless agree that the one thing that has remained constant throughout is the great care, love and service that is given to the residents, a tradition stretching back to the inception of the Home from its small beginnings in the 1840s.

In the nineteenth century most residents were in their sixties or seventies, broken down by poverty, hard lives and semi-starvation. The Home was a literal refuge from destitution, exposure, and hunger, a peaceful haven with a warm fireside and plentiful food, where residents could attend to their religious duties and draw their final breath surrounded by their fellow Jews. Today, in 2001, the average age of the residents is eighty-eight. They come to the Home because of its Jewish atmosphere, and to receive excellent nursing care and rehabilitation. Most who are able, find their last years in the home comfortable, dignified, and very stimulating.

What is perhaps most remarkable is the concept of the new, fulfilling, and exciting phase of life to be had at the Home once the storms of former days have been put behind. Life at the Home might be a last chapter of a life for many, but it is no anti-climax. In many respects the Home has been decades ahead of the psychologists who have taken until very recently to recognise that the mind (and indeed spirit) can continue to develop and change until an advanced age, unless other more dramatic events take over.

The political debate now centres upon the potential contribution charities (particularly religious-based charities) can make towards providing public services, using a combination of private and public funds – a concept that is nothing new to Nightingale.

The words of Dr. Bernard Brest the former Medical Officer of the

A NOTE ON SOURCES

The research and writing of this account has largely relied on printed sources. This is due to the fact that much of the original archives of the Home were lost in the flooding of a basement at Nightingale in the 1970s – a major loss. The only substantial early material in possession of the Home are the minutes of the Committee from 1903–1910 which cover the crucial move from the East End to Wandsworth and a miscellaneous collection of deeds, documents and photographs.

For the nineteenth century the *Jewish Chronicle* is a rich and most invaluable source. The reports about the charities in this period were voluminous and the paper also helpfully printed detailed summaries of many of the annual reports and meetings of the Homes.

From 1900 onwards there is a nearly complete run of annual reports on the Home, a detailed and largely accurate source of information.

I have been fortunate to be able to draw on oral history back to the 1920s, from a number of individuals associated with the Home. This has supplemented the drier facts of the printed sources and given a sounder human context for the information.

While there are relatively few books relevant to this area of study, V. D. Lipman's *A Century of Social Service 1859–1959. The Jewish Board of Guardians* has been of great help. There is also relevant material in the *Transactions of the Jewish Historical Society of England*, relating to S. A. Green and aspects of the earlier history of the constituent charities. Gerry Black's *Lord Rothschild and the Barber*, includes useful material and comparisons.

INDEX